大师经典文库

Confucius

论 语

The Analects

孔子　著

Arthur Waley　译

外语教学与研究出版社

（京）新登字 155 号

京权图字 01－97－1105

图书在版编目（CIP）数据

论语：汉英对照/（春秋）孔子著；（英）威利译．－北京：外语教学与研究出版社，1997.12
（大师经典文库）
ISBN 7－5600－1373－2

Ⅰ.论… Ⅱ.①孔… ②威… Ⅲ.英语-对照读物-汉、英 Ⅳ.H319.4:B

中国版本图书馆 CIP 数据核字(98)第 01432 号

大师经典文库
论 语
孔子 著

Arthur Waley 译

* * *

外语教学与研究出版社出版发行
（北京西三环北路 19 号）
北京外国语大学印刷厂印刷
新华书店总店北京发行所经销
开本 850×1168 1/32 9 印张
1998 年 9 月第 1 版 1998 年 9 月第 1 次印刷
印数：1—5000 册

* * *

ISBN 7－5600－1373－2
H·774
定价：10.90 元

The paper in this book is produced from pure wood
pulp, without the use of chlorine or any other substance
harmful to the environment. The energy used in its
production consists almost entirely of hydroelectricity
and heat generated from waste material, thereby
conserving fossil fuels and contributing little
to the greenhouse effect.

This edition published 1996 by Wordsworth Editions Limited
Cumberland House, Crib Street, Ware, Hertfordshire SG12 9ET

ISBN 1 85326 462 8

Typeset in Great Britain by Antony Gray
Printed and bound in Denmark by Nørhaven

出版说明

外语教学与研究出版社自９０年代以来，一直以促进国际文化交流为己任，致力于原版外语著作的引进、出版工作，逐步形成了规模化、系统化、精品化的出版传统，在广大读者中产生了一定的影响。当下，我国外语图书出版呈现出较为严重的不均衡局面，即文艺类图书品种相对齐全，而人文科学、社会科学类图书的出版却寥寥可数，远远滞后于日益增长的文化市场需求。为了填补这一空白，外研社决定编辑出版英文版哲学、社会科学类丛书"大师经典文库"，系统地推出一批世界著名思想家、哲学家、政治学家、历史学家、心理学家的经典学术名著，包括我国古代哲学典籍的权威英译本，为广大英语学习者提供高质量的阅读文本，也为各类社会科学研究工作者提供必备的学术资料。本丛书内容详实，制作精美，每一种均约请著名专家、学者专门撰写评介性的序言。外研社将本丛书的出版视做一项利国利民的文化基础工程，将坚持不懈地完善、充实它，希望它能够赢得读者朋友们的喜爱。

外语教学与研究出版社
1997 年 11 月

序　言

汤一介

　　孔子名丘，字仲尼，生于公元前551年，死于公元前479年，活到73岁。孔子的祖先是宋国的贵族，大约在孔子前几代就没落了，失去了贵族的地位。孔子年轻时做过几任小官，中年时曾做过三个月的鲁国司寇，相当于警察局长，晚年曾周游列国，但他一生大部分时间从事教育，教出不少有知识、有才能、有道德的学生。孔子是我国最早的、也是最有影响的思想家和教育家，两千多年来，人们都把他视为圣人。他为什么被尊为圣人？对中国文化的发展产生了多大的影响？

　　生活在春秋末期的孔子，并不像后来我国封建社会的统治者们所吹捧的那样，似乎是什么不食人间烟火的"文宣王"、"大成至圣先师"等等，他也是一个有血有肉的现实社会中的人。孔子很喜欢音乐，他在齐国听相传是虞舜时的"韶"乐，竟然多日无心品尝肉的美味，并且说："想不到音乐的高妙意境达到这种地步。"孔子对诗也有浓厚的兴趣，有一次他对他的学生说："年轻人呀！为什么不学诗？诗啊，可以振奋人的志气，可以观察事物的得失，可以和大家和睦相处，可以婉转地抒发心中的怨气。就近处说，可以知道如何孝顺父母；就远处说，可以懂得事奉君主，并且还能认识许多鸟兽草木之名。"孔子热心地学习各种礼仪，对于各种礼仪的规矩很了解，据《论语》记载，他到太庙参加祭祀鲁国先君的礼，每件事都要详细地询问，别人讥笑他，他听到后说："谨慎求教才是真正的礼。"孔子赞美他的学生颜回安于贫困说："颜回真是一个有贤德的人呀！一竹筒的饭，一瓢清水，

3

住在简陋的小房子里，别人都受不了这样穷苦的生活所带来的忧愁，颜回却不改变他自有的快乐。"可是孔子有时又追求富贵，奔走于权贵之门，国君召唤他，他等不及架好马车，就赶快跑去了。他吃饭也很讲究，饭要吃精米，肉要吃细肉丝。但孔子有时也把这些看得很淡，有一次他说："吃的是粗食，喝的是清水，困倦时弯着臂当枕头睡觉，这种日子也很有乐趣，用不正当的手段取富贵，对我来说，就好像是天空中飘浮的云一样。"孔子说过许多有道理的话，今天我们仍然把它们作为格言，如"学而不厌，诲人不倦"，"过而不改，是谓过矣"(有过错不能改，这是真正的过错)，"温故而知新"等等。但他也说过一些错话，如"唯女子与小人为难养也"(只有女人和小人难得和他们相处)。孔子对他的学生要求很严厉，批评起来不讲情面，他的学生宰予白天睡大觉，不好好学习，孔子批评说："腐朽的木头是不能雕琢的，粪土筑成的墙是无法涂抹得光滑洁白的。"而有时他对弟子们又非常亲切，他说颜回："我只看到你不断进步，而没有看到你停止不前。"孔子为人有时很豪放，他说他自己是"发愤忘食，乐以忘忧，不知老之将至"的人。可是有时在地位比他高的人面前，他又表现得谨小慎微，循规蹈矩，不敢超越那些世俗的礼仪。孔子的弟子都很尊敬他们的老师，但如果有意见也敢提出批评，孔子则或作解释或作自我批评。有一次，孔子到了武城地方，听到了鼓琴歌诗的声音。孔子微笑着说："宰一只小鸡，还用得着牛刀吗?"意思是，礼乐是治国平天下用的，在这样一个小城中推行，似乎是大题小作。他的弟子子游听了之后说："从前我听老师说过：君子懂得礼乐的道理就会爱护老百姓，民众懂得礼乐的道理社会就容易治理。"孔子立刻对随行的弟子们说："你们这几位学生呀，子游刚才说的是对的。我刚才说的不过是一句戏言罢了!"孔子也常和他的学生一起讨论问题,有一次他把几个得意的学生召在一起谈各自的志向,子路说他的志向是"愿意把自己的马车、衣服和朋友共同享受,就是用坏了也并不遗憾"。颜回说他的志向是"只想做到不夸耀自己的好处,不表白自己的功劳"。孔子则说,他愿意让"老者安之,朋友信之,少者怀之"。看来,孔子的人生境界确实比他的学生高。

从上面这些记载的事迹看,孔子并不像后来吹捧他的人所形容的那样,是一个道貌岸然的"超人",更不是一个天生的"神人",而是一个有感情、有抱负、有喜怒哀乐、有丰富知识的现实中的人。

如果孔子就像我们上面所描述的那样,大家就会说:看来,孔子并没有什么伟大之处,可是又为什么说他是一个伟大的思想家、教育家,而且对中国文化产生过那么大的影响,对世界文化也有不小影响,被推崇为世界十大思想家之一呢?当然,如果孔子只是如我上面所说,他确称不上伟大思想家和教育家。我之所以先对孔子作为一个"人"来作一番描述,目的是使大家知道他是一个"人"而不是"神"。但是,他又确实是一位伟大的思想家和教育家,关于这一点我们可以从《论语》一书记载的孔子的言行中得到证实。为此,下面我们要介绍一下《论语》这部书,并根据这部书来阐述孔子的思想。

《论语》是记载孔子及其弟子言行的一部书。据《汉书·艺文志》说:"《论语》者,孔子应答弟子、时人及弟子相与而接闻于夫子之语也。"《论语》在汉朝有三种不同的本子:《鲁论语》、《齐论语》和《古文论语》。到西汉末年,由张禹根据《鲁论语》并参考了《齐论语》校定成书,就是我们今天看到的《论语》本子。《论语》共20篇二万余字。从汉朝起,《论语》

和《孝经》就是人们初学的必读书，然后人们才学习儒家的经典《易经》、《诗经》、《书经》、《礼记》、《春秋》等。《论语》古今的注释非常之多，据日本学者林泰辅《论语年谱》所著录，关于《论语》的著作有三千多种，当然还有他未曾见到的，就更无法统计了。《论语》主要的注本有《论语注疏》(何晏集解，邢日丙疏，收在《十三经注疏》中)，《论语集注》(在朱熹的《四书解注》中)，刘宝楠的《论语正义》，现在有中华书局出版的杨伯峻《论语译注》，是一本对初学《论语》很有帮助的书，但蔡尚思近年在巴蜀出版社出版的《论语》(导读)对杨书有所批评，可以参考。

《论语》的内容非常丰富，古今中外学者对它已经作过多方面多视角的研究，如果我要把它所包含的思想内容方方面面都一一介绍，决不是一两万字可以做到的。因此，这里我只能根据《论语》，并参考少量其他材料，对作为一位伟大思想家和教育家的孔子作一简要介绍。

我们从孔子作为一位伟大思想家看，根据《论语》可以把他的学说叫作"仁学"。据杨伯峻先生《论语译注》统计，在《论语》中，孔子讲"仁"的地方共109次，当然讲到"礼"的地方也不少，共75次。孔子提出"仁"的概念可以说是他全部思想的核心，它是"礼"的根本内涵，是伦理道德的基本根据，是做人的根本道理，是人们应该追求的最高境界。根据现存史料，在孔子以前没有人把"仁"作为一最高哲学概念提出来过。孔子提出"仁"的概念并不是偶然的，它在一定程度上反映了春秋时代社会发展的状况。春秋时期，铁器开始应用于农业生产，生产力发展了，私田扩大了，因此产生了一个新问题：如何使失去生产兴趣的劳动者对生产有点积极性，不再逃亡，使他们能"近者悦，远者来"（使近处的老百姓感到喜悦，远方的人也闻讯而来）（《子路》），以适应生产发展的需要。同时，周天子势力衰落，诸侯竞起，统治者内部矛盾重重，战争不断。这一时期，"弑君三十六，亡国五十二，诸侯奔走不得保其社稷者不可胜数"。在这种情况下，孔子为了适应当时的社会生活的要求，致力于恢复"礼乐制度"，以便使社会平稳地过渡到一个新的"天下有道"的社会。因此，孔子提出来，应该把他人当成"人"看。他的学生问他什么是"仁"，他回答说："爱人。"别看只是简单的两个字，这两个字包涵的意义重大。"爱人"，对劳动者来说，就是统治者也应把劳动者当"人"来爱护。对调整统治者的内部关系说，就是要"克己复礼"。

孔子曾经说过"苛政猛于虎"。据《礼记·檀引》记载，有一天孔子经过泰山，有一妇女在坟边哭得很伤心，孔子要子路去问明原因，那妇女说，他的公公、丈夫和儿子都被老虎害了。孔子问她：为什么不早些离开呢？妇女回答说：因为这里没有苛政。于是孔子对他的弟子说："你们记住，苛政猛于虎。"可见孔子主张应该爱护老百姓。孔子教导他的弟子说："一个人应该普遍地关怀老百姓，并且亲近有仁德的人。"（"泛爱众而亲仁。"）（《学而》）这句话明显地表现了孔子对人的关怀。他认为这样才可以达到"宽以得众"，"惠足以使人"的目的。为政者能宽能惠，这样老百姓才会归顺你。

本自西周以来，在统治者内部都要实行"礼乐之治"，但到孔子时已经"礼坏乐崩"了。为什么"礼坏乐崩"了呢？照孔子看，这是由于"礼乐"已失去了一种内在的精神，所以孔子说："一个人如果没有仁爱之心，那礼对他又能如何呢？一个人如果没有仁爱之心，那乐对他又有什么用呢？"（"人而不仁，如礼何？人而不仁，如乐何?")（《八佾》）因此，孔子反对把"礼乐"仅仅当作一种形式，他说："现在所说的礼呀! 难道只是指玉帛一类的礼器吗? 现在所说的乐呀! 难道只是指钟鼓一类的乐器吗?"（"礼云礼云，玉帛云乎哉! 乐云乐云，钟鼓云乎哉!"（《阳货》）这就是说"礼乐"如果离开了"仁爱"的精神，那就如同把"礼乐"看成玉帛和钟鼓一类物质的东西而失去其内在精神了。从这里看，孔子把"仁"看得比"礼乐"更重要，他认为应用一种"仁爱"的精神来讲"礼乐"，以便"礼乐"具有"爱人"的精神内涵。颜回问孔子什么是"仁"，孔子回答说："克己复礼为仁，一日克己复礼，天下归仁焉，为仁由己，而由人乎?"（《颜渊》）克制自己的私心，使自己的言行符合"礼"的要求，这就是"仁"了。一旦做到了，天下的人就会称许你是仁德的人。所以做到"仁"，完全靠自己，哪里能靠别人呢?这就是说，要做到仁，要注意两个方面：首先要"克己"，就是要对自己有个要求，要推己及人，应该"己所不欲，勿施于人"；其次要"复礼"，为了推行"仁"又必须有个规范，这就必须用"礼"作为规矩来约束人的言行。所以颜回问如何操作时，孔子说："非礼勿视，非礼勿听，非礼勿言，非礼勿动。"孔子的这几句话是有毛病的，它会把人的创造性、主动性大大限制住。如果我们说，这里的"礼"是要有"仁"的内涵，即"爱人"的精神规范，那或者从某一角度看也许还有一点意义。但我认为，孔子的"克己"包含有自觉性的意义，所以孔子说："为仁由己，而由人乎哉!"孔子又说："仁离我们很远吗?我们只要一心向仁，这仁爱之心就立刻会涌现出来。"（《述而》）这就是说，"仁"本来是自己内在的品德，只要你去发挥它，爱人的精神就会表现出来。孔子这一强调人的自觉性的思想对以后中国社会文化有着非常大的影响。

孔子的"仁学"还有一个比较重要的思想，就是"尚贤"。

所谓"尚贤"，就是要注重一个人的道德、学问和才能，而不要去更多地考虑其出身的高低。关于"尚贤"，孔子讲过许多话，如他说"举贤才"，又说"学也禄在其中"(有知识有学问就可以得到丰厚的俸禄)(《卫灵公》)，"学而优则仕"(《子张》)等等。在孔子看来，要做官就应该有知识、有学问。这个看法，对以后中国社会影响很大，从积极方面说，它打破了贵族垄断做官的权力；但从消极方面看，会被利用作为"读书做官"的根据。在《论语》中记载着这样一个故事：子路让孔了的另外一个学生子羔去做费这个地方的官，孔子对子路说："你这是害人家的孩子。"子路说："这个地方有老百姓，有土地和五谷，何必一定要读书才叫有学问呢?"孔子批评子路说："我就讨厌像你这样强嘴利舌的人。"(《先进》)孔子认为，没有道德、学问和才能的统治者，那只能是害人的统治者。所以当他的学生冉雍问他如何处理好政事时，孔子说："带头工作，原谅别人的小过错，提拔有道德、有学问和有才能的人。"("先有司，赦小过，举贤才。")(《子路》)有了好的统治者，才能把国家治理好，将人民管理好，社会才可以安定。

在《论语》中，孔子和他的弟子讨论"仁"的地方很多，看来孔子的"仁"意义很广泛，几乎包括做人的全部道理。例如子张问孔子怎样才算是"仁"，孔子说："能有五种品德于天下，就算是仁了。"子张又问，是哪五种美德呢?孔子说："就是恭、宽、仁、敏、惠。凡能行事恭敬就不会受轻侮，能行事宽厚就会得到民众的拥护，做事守信就会受到人们的信任，能勤奋进取就容易成功，能施恩惠于民就会得民心。"(《阳货》)又如孔子说："仁者必有勇，勇者不必有仁。"(《宪问》)甚至孔子认为，应当行"仁"的时候，对老师也不必讲谦让。这就是说，孔子认为，行"仁"是义不容辞的，应该"无求生以害仁，有杀身以成仁"（《卫灵公》）。这种为一种理想而牺牲的精神，对中国人也有很大影响，例如，文天祥在他临刑时的衣带上写着："孔曰成仁，孟曰取义，唯其尽义，所以至人，读圣贤书，所学何事，而今而后，庶几无愧。"

孔子认为，你要想发挥你"仁爱"的品德，那你就应该去追求"仁"的境界。"仁"是自己的内在品德，只能靠自己发挥它，它不是外在力量可以使你得到的。孔子说："人能弘道，非道弘人。"（《卫灵公》）这里的"道"就是"为仁之学"，也就是"为人之道"。"仁道"要靠人来发扬光大的，如果人不努力"尚仁"，不自觉地追求"仁"，那么"仁道"也不会自动地使人成为有道德、有学问的完美的人。这里，我们可以看出，孔子非常强调人的自觉性和主动性。孔子很看不惯那些不努力学习、不求上进的人，认为这样的人没有出息，他说："年轻人是可畏的，哪里敢断定他们将来的成就不如现在的我们呢？但是他们如果不努力，到了四五十岁，仍然没有什么表现，一无所成，这样的人也就不值得敬畏了。"（《子罕》）由于孔子重视人自身的努力，相对地说这也就降低了西周以来对"天"的崇拜的作用，也可以说是在一定程度上从某个方面对于把"天"看作主宰力量的否定。

孔子不仅是伟大的思想家，而且是个伟大的教育家，他的教育是为了实现他的"仁学"理想，为了培养人"成圣成贤"。他从长期的教育实践中总结了很多有意义、有启发性的教育思想和求得知识的方法。孔子提出"有教无类"，这句话虽然有不同的解释，但它包含要扩大教育面、使受教育的人不仅仅限于贵族的意思，应该是无疑的。孔子自己实践了他的"有教无类"的主张，所以他说："只要给我十条干肉作学费，我从来没有不教诲的。"（《述而》）他的教育活动，结束了过去由贵族垄断的官府之学，开始了学问的私家传授。

孔子通过他的长期教育实践活动总结出了不少有益的教育方法，今天看来仍然具有重要意义。首先，孔子比较强调人的知识、学问来源于学习。在《论语》中，我们也可以看到孔子讲到过"生知"、"唯上智与下愚不移"等等。但他实际上并不重视这些。孔子从来没有认为他自己是"上智"的人，他说："我非生而知之者，而是喜欢古代文化，勤奋敏捷求得知识的人。"（《述而》）孔子非常好学，他给自己的评论是："只有十户人家的小地方，其中必有忠信像我一样的人，但决没有像我这样好学的人。"（"十室之邑，必有忠信，如丘焉。不如丘之好学也。"）（《公冶长》）可见孔子非常重视学习。他主张学习的内容大体有两方面：

一是从学习古代文献和典章制度方面得来的知识。这里所说的"古代文献"就是《诗》、《书》、《礼》、《乐》等古代经典。二是从现实生活中得到的知识。这可以说是现实知识。

在《论语》中记载着孔子说的在现实中要注意学习的话，如他说："多方听取意见，然后选择其中最好的跟着学，多多地观察而默记于心。"（"多闻择其善者而从之，多见而识之。"）（《述而》）"三人在一起，其中必定有可以做我老师的，选择他们的长处跟着学，看到他们的缺点就自我警惕来改正自己。"（"三人行，必有我师焉，择其善者而从之，其不善者而改之。"）（《述而》）"敏而好学，不耻下问。"（《公冶长》）等等。但孔子轻视种菜、种庄稼，则是不可取的。

其次，孔子对学习规律作了很好的概括，得出一些认识事物的规律和学习方法，并以此指导他的学生学习。他提出反复地学习可以加深人们的认识，获得新的知识，他说"学而时习之"，"温故而知新"等，就是这个意思。孔子还从教育实践中总结出"学"和"思"的关系，"学"是学习前人的经验(从历史文献中学)和从生活实践中学；"思"是把前人的经验和生活中得到的经验通过思考加以消化，使之成为自己的知识。所以他认为：只学习前人的知识而自己不思考，将会停留在迷惘之中而不知道正确与错误；只是凭空思想而不利用前人的知识和经验，那就会一无所成。"学而不思则罔，思而不学则殆。"（《为政》）看来，虽然孔子也重视"思"，但孔子教学生更重视"学"，他认为"学"是"思"的基础，所以他说："我曾一整天不吃饭、一整夜不睡觉去思考，可是没有什么收获，还不如努力去学点什么。"（"吾尝终日不食，终夜不寝，以思，无益，不如学也。"）（《卫灵公》）孔子认为，知识应该尽可能丰富，他自己就是一个博学多能的人，但是渊博的学问必须有个中心思想来贯穿，这就是他所说的"一以贯之"。抓住了贯穿一切的"一"（根本道理），才能把许多表面上看起来不连贯的知识贯穿起来。根据孔子整个思想看，这个贯穿一切的"一"就是"忠恕之道"。而"忠恕之道"正是"仁"的表现，所以归根到底就是"仁"了。他说："君子没有一顿饭的时间违背仁，在仓卒忙乱的时候必须如此，在颠沛流离的时候也必须如此。"（"君子无终食之间违仁，造次必于是，颠沛必于是。"）（《里仁》）照孔子看，一切都应以能否符合"仁"的标准为要求，任何人对自己都要有个要求，把自己看成个"人"，尽自己的责任，讲究个做人的道理。

第三，孔子的教育思想中还包含着学习态度的问题。有一次孔子对他的学生子路说："子路呀！我教导你，知道吗？自己确实知道的才是知道，不知道的就承认自己不知道，这样才是知的态度。"（"由!诲汝知之乎!知之为知之，不知为不知，是知也。"）（《为政》）他教学生也颇注意"因材施教"，如果你读《论语》，可以看到孔子的学生向他问"仁"、问"政"、问"知"的地方很多，他往往都是根据不同的对象给以不同的回答。为此，孔子在教学中比较注重启发式，他说："教育学生，不到他苦思苦想而仍然领会不了的时候，不去开导他；不到他想说而说不出来的时候，不去启发他。教他一个方面，他不能由此推知其他几个方面，就不再去教他新的内容。"（"不愤，不启；不悱，不发；举一隅不以三隅反，则不复也。"）（《述而》）孔子采用这样的方法，去推动学生思考问题，主动地学习。

两千多年过去了，我们今天研究孔子的思想，不能不承认中国文化在许多方面都受到孔子思想的影响。他在中国文化史上确实是一位具有开创性的伟大思想家、伟大教育家。《论语》这部书不能不说是中华民族文化精神的宝贵财富，它给人们许多有意义的启迪和智慧，以及做人的道理。它对中国社会曾经产生过超过其他著作的影响，而且今后仍然会对中国社会文化生产发生无可置疑的作用。同时，我也相信《论语》这部书对世界各国人民同样会是一本有意义的教材。

　　注：本文中的译文参考了杨伯峻先生的《论语译注》。

论 语

THE ANALECTS

学而第一

（一）

子曰："学而时习之，不亦悦乎？有朋自远方来，不亦乐乎？人不知而不愠，不亦君子乎？"

（二）

有子曰："其为人也孝悌，而好犯上者，鲜矣。不好犯上而好作乱者，未之有也。君子务本，本立而道生。孝悌也者，其仁之本与？"

（三）

子曰："巧言令色，鲜矣仁。"

BOOK ONE

1   The Master said, To learn and at due times to repeat what one has learnt, is that not after all[1] a pleasure? That friends should come to one from afar,[2] is this not after all delightful? To remain unsoured even though one's merits are unrecognised by others, is that not after all what is expected of a gentleman?

2   Master Yu said, Those who in private life behave well towards their parents and elder brothers, in public life seldom show a disposition to resist the authority of their superiors. And as for such men starting a revolution, no instance of it has ever occurred. It is upon the trunk[3] that a gentleman works. When that is firmly set up, the Way grows. And surely proper behaviour towards parents and elder brothers is the trunk of Goodness?

3   The Master said, 'Clever talk and a pretentious manner'[4] are seldom found in the Good.

1   The 'after all' implies 'even though one does not hold office'.
2   Several of the disciples belonged to other States (e.g. Wei and Ch'i); but there is no evidence that they came to Lu on account of Confucius. Unless, however, there is here some allusion that escapes us, the phrase must refer to the visits of admirers from abroad, perhaps friends made during the Master's journeys in Honan.
3   i.e. upon what is fundamental, as opposed to 'the twigs', i.e. small arts and accomplishments, which the gentleman leaves to his inferiors.
4   Traditional phrase. cf. *Shu Ching*, Kao Yao Mo.

（四）

　　曾子曰：　"吾日三省吾身。为人谋，而不忠乎？与朋友交，而不信乎？传，不习乎？"

（五）

　　子曰：　"道千乘之国，敬事而信，节用而爱人，使民以时。"

（六）

　　子曰：　"弟子入则孝，出则悌，谨而信，泛爱众而亲仁。行有余力，则以学文。"

（七）

　　子夏曰：　"贤贤易色；事父母能竭其力，事君能致其身；与朋友交；言而有信。虽曰未学，吾必谓之学矣。"

4   Master Tsêng said, Every day I examine myself on these three
     points: in acting on behalf of others, have I always been loyal to
     their interests? In intercourse with my friends, have I always been
     true to my word? Have I failed to repeat[1] the precepts that have
     been handed down to me?

5   The Master said, A country of a thousand war-chariots cannot be
     administered unless the ruler attends strictly to business, punctually
     observes his promises, is economical in expenditure, shows
     affection towards his subjects in general, and uses the labour of
     the peasantry only at the proper times of year.[2]

6   The Master said, A young man's duty is to behave well to his
     parents at home and to his elders abroad, to be cautious in giving
     promises and punctual in keeping them, to have kindly feelings
     towards everyone, but seek the intimacy of the Good. If, when
     all that is done, he has any energy to spare, then let him study the
     polite arts.[3]

7   Tzu-hsia said, A man who

> Treats his betters as betters,
> Wears an air of respect,
> Who into serving father and mother
> Knows how to put his whole strength,
> Who in the service of his prince will lay down his life,
> Who in intercourse with friends is true to his word –

others may say of him that he still lacks education,[4] but I for my
part should certainly call him an educated man.

1   And so keep in memory.
2   i.e. not when they ought to be working in the fields. Bad rulers, on the
     contrary, listen to music or go hunting when they ought to be
     attending to business, continually employ labour on ostentatious
     building-schemes, etc.
3   i.e. learn to recite the *Songs*, practise archery, deportment, and the like.
4   i.e. knowledge of ritual, precedents, the correct use on social occasions
     of verse from the *Songs*, etc.

（八）

子曰：“君子不重则不威，学则不固。主忠信。无友不好己者。过则勿惮改。”

（九）

曾子曰：“慎终追远，民德归厚矣。”

（十）

子禽问于子贡曰：“夫子至于是邦也，必闻其政，求之与？抑与之与？”子贡曰：“夫子温、良、恭、俭、让以得之。夫子之求之也，其诸异乎人之求之与！”

（十一）

子曰：“父在观其志，父没观其行，三年无改于父之道，可谓孝矣。”

8   The Master said, If a gentleman is frivolous,[1] he will lose the respect of his inferiors and lack firm ground[2] upon which to build up his education. First and foremost he must learn to be faithful to his superiors, to keep promises, to refuse the friendship of all who are not like him.[3] And if he finds he has made a mistake, then he must not be afraid of admitting the fact and amending his ways.

9   Master Tsêng said, When proper respect towards the dead is shown at the End and continued after they are far away the moral force (*te*) of a people has reached its highest point.

10 Tzu-Ch'in[4] said to Tzu-kung, When our Master arrives in a fresh country he always manages to find out about its policy.[5] Does he do this by asking questions, or do people tell him of their own accord? Tzu-kung said, Our Master gets things by being cordial, frank, courteous, temperate, deferential. That is our Master's way of enquiring – a very different matter,[6] certainly, from the way in which enquiries are generally made.

11 The Master said, While a man's father is alive, you can only see his intentions; it is when his father dies that you discover whether or not he is capable of carrying them out. If for the whole three years of mourning he manages to carry on the household exactly as in his father's day, then he is a good son indeed.

1   i.e. irresponsible and unreliable in his dealings with others.
2   The sentence runs awkwardly and is probably corrupt.
3   i.e. of those who still reckon in terms of 'profit and loss', and have taken *jen* (Goodness) as standard.
4   Disciple of Confucius. See XVI, and XIX, 25.
5   Not, of course, about the details of administration, but about the secret, general maxims which inspire the ruler.
6   The double particle *ch'i-chu*, peculiar to the *Analects* and *Kungyang Chuan*, does not seem to differ in meaning from the ordinary modal *ch'i*.

（十二）

有子曰：“礼之用，和为贵。先王之道斯为美；小大由之。有所不行，知和而和，不以礼节之，亦不可行也。”

（十三）

有子曰：“信近于义，言可复也。恭近于礼，远耻辱也。因不失其亲，亦可宗也。”

（十四）

子曰：“君子食无求饱，居无求安，敏于事而慎于言，就有道而正焉，可谓好学也已。”

（十五）

子贡曰：“贫而无谄，富而无骄，何如？”子曰：“可也。未若贫而乐道，富而好礼者也。”子贡曰：

12 Master Yu said, In the usages of ritual it is harmony[1] that is prized; the Way of the Former Kings from this[2] got its beauty. Both small matters and great depend upon it. If things go amiss, he who knows the harmony[3] will be able to attune them. But if harmony itself is not modulated by ritual, things will still go amiss.

13 Master Yu said,

> In your promises cleave to what is right,
> And you will be able to fulfil your word.
> In your obeisances cleave to ritual,
> And you will keep dishonour at bay.
> Marry one who has not betrayed her own kin,
> And you may safely present her to your Ancestors.[4]

14 The Master said, A gentleman who never goes on eating till he is sated, who does not demand comfort in his home, who is diligent in business and cautious in speech, who associates with those that possess the Way and thereby corrects his own faults – such a one may indeed be said to have a taste for learning.

15 Tzu-kung said, 'Poor without cadging, rich without swagger.' What of that?[5] The Master said, Not bad. But better still, 'Poor, yet delighting in the Way, rich, yet a student of ritual.' Tzu-kung said, The saying of the *Songs*,[6]

1 Harmony between man and nature; playing the musical mode that harmonises with the season, wearing seasonable clothes, eating seasonable food, and the like.
2 i.e. from harmony.
3 i.e. the act that harmonises with the moment.
4 Lines 2, 4, and 6 rhyme. For the last rhyme, which belongs to a well-established type, see Karlgren, *The Rimes in the Sung section of the Shi King*.
5 i.e. what of it as a motto?
6 *The Book of Songs* p. 46, which describes the elegance of a lover. Tzu-kung interprets it as describing the pains the gentleman has taken to improve his character, and suggests that Confucius prefers the second maxim ('Poor, yet delighting . . .') because it implies a greater effort of self-improvement.

"《诗》云：'如切如磋，如琢如磨。'其斯之谓
与？"子曰："赐也！始可与言《诗》已矣，告诸往
而知来者。"

（十六）

子曰："不患人之不己知，患不知人也。"

> As thing cut, as thing filed,
> As thing chiselled, as thing polished

refers, I suppose, to what you have just said? The Master said, Ssu, now I can really begin to talk to you about the *Songs,* for when I allude to sayings of the past, you see what bearing they have on what was to come after.

16 The Master said, (The good man) does not grieve that other people do not recognise his merits. His only anxiety is lest he should fail to recognise theirs.

为政第二

（一）

子曰：“为政以德，譬如北辰，居其所而众星共之。”

（二）

子曰：“《诗》三百，一言以蔽之，曰：‘思无邪’。”

（三）

子曰：“道之以政，齐之以刑，民免而无耻；道之以德，齐之以礼，有耻且格。”

（四）

子曰：“吾十有五而志乎学，三十而立，四十而不惑，五十而知天命，六十而耳顺，七十而从心所欲不逾矩。”

BOOK TWO

1 The Master said, He who rules by moral force (*te*) is like the pole-star, which remains in its place while all the lesser stars do homage to it.

2 The Master said, If out of the three hundred *Songs* I had to take one phrase to cover all my teaching, I would say 'Let there be no evil in your thoughts.'[1]

3 The Master said, Govern the people by regulations, keep order among them by chastisements, and they will flee from you, and lose all self-respect. Govern them by moral force, keep order among them by ritual and they will keep their self-respect and come to you of their own accord.

4 The Master said, At fifteen I set my heart upon learning. At thirty, I had planted my feet firm upon the ground. At forty, I no longer suffered from perplexities. At fifty, I knew what were the biddings of Heaven. At sixty, I heard them with docile ear. At seventy, I could follow the dictates of my own heart; for what I desired no longer overstepped the boundaries of right.

---

1 *The Book of Songs*, p. 275, l. 7, where however *ssu* does not mean 'thoughts', but is an exclamation, 'oh', 'ah', or the like; but in applying ancient texts it is the words themselves that matter, not the context; and these words can be reapplied in any sense which they are conceivably capable of bearing.

（五）

孟懿子问孝，子曰："无违。"樊迟御，子告之曰："孟孙问孝于我，我对曰无违。"樊迟曰："何谓也？"子曰："生，事之以礼；死，葬之以礼，祭之以礼。"

（六）

孟武伯问孝，子曰："父母唯其疾之忧。"

（七）

子游问孝，子曰："今之孝者，是谓能养。至于犬马，皆能有养，不敬，何以别乎？"

（八）

子夏问孝，子曰："色难。有事，弟子服其劳；有酒食，先生馔。曾是以为孝乎？"

5   Mêng I Tzu[1] asked about the treatment of parents. The Master
     said, Never disobey! When Fan Ch'ih[2] was driving his carriage
     for him, the Master said, Mêng asked me about the treatment of
     parents and I said, Never disobey! Fan Ch'ih said, In what sense
     did you mean it? The Master said, While they are alive, serve
     them according to ritual. When they die, bury them according to
     ritual and sacrifice to them according to ritual.[3]

6   Mêng Wu Po[4] asked about the treatment of parents. The Master
     said, Behave in such a way that your father and mother have no
     anxiety about you, except concerning your health.

7   Tzu-Yu asked about the treatment of parents. The Master said,
     'Filial sons' nowadays are people who see to it that their parents
     get enough to eat. But even dogs and horses are cared for to that
     extent. If there is no feeling of respect, wherein lies the
     difference?

8   Tzu-hsia asked about the treatment of parents. The Master said,
     It is the demeanour[5] that is difficult. Filial piety does not consist
     merely in young people undertaking the hard work, when
     anything has to be done, or serving their elders first with wine
     and food. It is something much more than that.

1   A young grandee of Lu, whose father sent him to study with
     Confucius. He died in 481 BC.
2   A disciple.
3   Evidently by 'disobey' Confucius meant 'disobey the rituals'. The reply
     was intended to puzzle the enquirer and make him think. In *Mencius*,
     III, A, 2, 'While they are alive . . .', etc., is given as a saying of Master
     Tsêng. Here and elsewhere 'sacrifice' means offerings in general and
     not only animal-sacrifice.
4   Son of Mêng I Tzu.
5   This is Chêng Hsüan's interpretation. Pao Hsien (6 BC–AD 65) takes *sê*
     to mean the expression of one's parents, which must be watched for
     hints of approval or disapproval.

（九）

子曰： "吾与回信，终日不违如愚。退而省其私，亦足以发，回也不愚。"

（十）

子曰： "视其所以，观其所由，察其所安，人焉廋哉，人焉廋哉？"

（十一）

子曰： "温故而知新，可以为师矣。"

（十二）

子曰： "君子不器。"

（十三）

子贡问君子，子曰： "先行其言而后从之。"

（十四）

子曰： "君子周而不比，小人比而不周。"

9   The Master said, I can talk to Yen Hui[1] a whole day without his ever differing from me. One would think he was stupid. But if I enquire into his private conduct when he is not with me I find that it fully demonstrates what I have taught him. No, Hui is by no means stupid.

10   The Master said, Look closely into his aims, observe the means by which he pursues them, discover what brings him content – and can the man's real worth[2] remain hidden from you, can it remain hidden from you?

11   The Master said, He who by reanimating[3] the Old can gain knowledge of the New is fit to be a teacher.

12   The Master said, A gentleman is not an implement.[4]

13   Tzu-kung asked about the true gentleman. The Master said, He does not preach what he practises till he has practised what he preaches.

14   The Master said, A gentleman can see a question from all sides without bias. The small man is biased and can see a question only from one side.

1   The favourite disciple. His early death is several times referred to in this book. It would be possible to put this passage in the past and suppose it to have been spoken after Yen Hui's death; but I see no reason to do so.

2   i.e. whether he is fit to be entrusted with office. There is no need to have seen him actually handling practical issues. cf. *Mencius*, IV, A, 15.

3   Literally, 'warming up'. The business of the teacher is to give fresh life to the Scriptures by reinterpreting them so that they apply to the problems of modern life. All scriptures (Homer, the *Koran*, our own Bible) have been used in this way. I have seen 'The poor ye have always with you' used as an argument against slum-clearance. We have read above how Tzu-kung showed himself to be a true teacher by 'reanimating' a passage from the *Songs*.

4   i.e. a specialist, a tool used for a special purpose. He need only have general, moral qualifications.

（十五）

子曰：“学而不思则罔，思而不学则殆。”

（十六）

子曰：“攻乎异端，斯害也已。”

（十七）

子曰：“由，诲汝知之乎？知之为知之，不知为不知，是知也。”

（十八）

子张学干禄，子曰：“多闻阙疑，慎言其余，则寡尤；多见阙殆，慎行其余，则寡悔。言寡尤，行寡悔，禄在其中矣。”

15 The Master said, 'He who learns but does not think, is lost.' He who thinks but does not learn is in great danger.[1]

16 The Master said, He who sets to work upon a different strand destroys the whole fabric.[2]

17 The Master said, Yu,[3] shall I teach you what knowledge is? When you know a thing, to recognise that you know it, and when you do not know a thing, to recognise that you do not know it. That is knowledge.[4]

18 Tzu-chang was studying the *Song* Han-lu.[5] The Master said, Hear much, but maintain silence[6] as regards doubtful points and be cautious in speaking of the rest; then you will seldom get into trouble. See much, but ignore what it is dangerous to have seen, and be cautious in acting upon the rest; then you will seldom want to undo your acts. He who seldom gets into trouble about what he has said and seldom does anything that he afterwards wishes he had not done, will be sure incidentally[7] to get his reward.

1 I imagine that the first clause is a proverbial saying, and that Confucius meets it with the second clause. The proverb says: 'To learn without thinking is fatal.' Confucius says: To think but not to learn (i.e. study the Way of the ancients) is equally dangerous.

2 The metaphor is one of weaving or netting. 'Strand' (*tuan*) is a sprout, something that sticks out, and so 'the loose end of a thread'. The moral Way as opposed to the opportunist Way of the World must be followed consistently. It is no use working at it in disconnected patches.

3 Familiar name of the disciple Tzu-lu.

4 That knowledge consists in knowing that one does not know is a frequent theme in early Chinese texts. cf. *Tao Te Ching*, ch. 71.

5 *The Book of Songs*, p. 213. It puns on Han-lu, the name of a mountain, and *han-lu* 'seeking princely rewards, preferment.'

6 Literally, 'leave a gap', a metaphor derived from the language of copyists and scribes. cf. XV, 25.

7 See additional notes. From 'Hear much' to 'acts' is in rhyme, but would be awkward to print as verse.

（十九）

　　哀公问曰："何为则民服？"孔子对曰："举直错诸枉，则民服；举枉错诸直，则民不服。"

（二十）

　　季康子问："使民敬、忠以劝，如之何？"子曰："临之以庄，则敬；孝慈，则忠；举善而教不能，则民劝。"

（二十一）

　　或谓孔子曰："子奚不为政？"子曰："《书》云：'孝乎惟孝，友于兄弟。'施于有政，是亦为政，奚其为为政？"

（二十二）

　　子曰："人而无信，不知其可也。大车无輗，小车无軏，其何以行之哉？"

19 Duke Ai[1] asked, What can I do in order to get the support of the common people? Master K'ung[2] replied, If you 'raise up the straight and set them on top of the crooked,' the commoners will support you. But if you raise the crooked and set them on top of the straight, the commoners will not support you.

20 Chi K'ang-tzu[3] asked whether there were any form of encouragement by which he could induce the common people to be respectful and loyal. The Master said, Approach them with dignity, and they will respect you. Show piety towards your parents and kindness towards your children, and they will be loyal to you. Promote those who are worthy, train those who are incompetent; that is the best form of encouragement.

21 Someone, when talking to Master K'ung, said, How is it that you are not in the public service? The Master said, The Book[4] says: 'Be filial, only be filial and friendly towards your brothers, and you will be contributing to government.' There are other sorts of service quite different from what you[5] mean by service.

22 The Master said, I do not see what use a man can be put to, whose word cannot be trusted. How can a waggon be made to go if it has no yoke-bar or a carriage, if it has no collar-bar?

1 Duke of Lu from 494-468 BC.
2 i.e. Confucius.
3 Head of the three families who were *de facto* rulers of Lu. Died 469 BC.
4 i.e. what Europeans call the *Book of History*. The passage does not occur in the genuine books. What it meant in its original context no doubt was 'Be pious to your ancestors . . . be generous in rewarding your officers of State.' Confucius 'reanimates' the ancient text, in order to prove that a virtuous private life makes a real contribution towards the public welfare.
5 *Ch'i* corresponds to the Latin *iste*.

（二十三）

子张问："十世可知也？"子曰："殷因于夏礼，所损益可知也。周因于殷礼，所损益可知也。其或继周者，虽百世可知也。"

（二十四）

子曰："非其鬼而祭之，谄也。见义不为，无勇也。"

23 Tzu-chang asked whether the state of things[1] ten generations hence could be foretold. The Master said, We know in what ways the Yin modified ritual when they followed upon the Hsia.[2] We know in what ways the Chou[3] modified ritual when they followed upon the Yin.[4] And hence we can foretell what the successors of Chou will be like, even supposing they do not appear till a hundred generations from now.

24 The Master said, Just as to sacrifice to ancestors other than one's own is presumption, so to see what is right and not do it is cowardice.

1   As regards ritual.
2   Supposed to have ruled in the 3rd and 2nd millennia BC.
3   The dynasty which still had a nominal hegemony in the time of Confucius.
4   The fall of Yin took place in the eleventh century BC. It was on the site of one of their capitals that the famous 'Honan oracle-bones' were found.

八佾第三

（一）

孔子谓：，"季氏八佾舞于庭，是可忍也，孰不可忍也。"

（二）

三家者以《雍》彻。子曰： "'相维辟公，天子穆穆'，奚取于三家之堂？"

（三）

子曰： "人而不仁，如礼何？人而不仁，如乐何？"

（四）

林放问礼之本。子曰： "大哉问！礼，与其奢也，宁俭；丧，与其易也，宁戚。"

BOOK THREE

1   Master K'ung said of the head of the Chi family[1] when he had
    eight teams[2] of dancers performing in his courtyard, If this man
    can be endured, who cannot be endured!

2   The Three Families used the *Yung Song*[3] during the removal of
    the sacrificial vessels. The Master said,

> By rulers and lords attended,
> The Son of Heaven, mysterious –

What possible application can such words have in the hall of the
Three Families?

3   The Master said, A man who is not Good, what can he have to
    do with ritual? A man who is not Good, what can he have to do
    with music?

4   Lin Fang asked for some main principles in connection with
    ritual. The Master said, A very big question. In ritual at large it is
    a safe rule always to be too sparing rather than too lavish; and in
    the particular case of mourning-rites, they should be dictated by
    grief rather than by fear.

1   One of the Three Families that had usurped most of the powers of the
    Duke of Lu.
2   See additional notes.
3   'He comes in solemn state . . .', *The Book of Songs*, p. 231. Its use was
    obviously only appropriate at the Emperor's Court. It would have been
    out of place at the Duke's palace, and was still more so in the hall of the
    Three Families.

（五）

子曰：　"夷狄之有君，不如诸夏之亡也。"

（六）

季氏旅于泰山。子谓冉有曰：　"汝弗能救与？"
对曰：　"不能。"子曰：　"呜呼！曾谓泰山不如林放
乎？"

（七）

子曰："君子无所争，必也射乎？揖让而升下，
而饮，其争也君子。"

5   The Master said, The barbarians of the East and North have retained their princes. They are not in such a state of decay as we in China.[1]

6   The head of the Chi family was going to make the offerings on Mount T'ai.[2] The Master said to Jan Ch'iu,[3] Cannot you save him from this? Jan Ch'iu replied, I cannot. The Master said, Alas, we can hardly suppose Mount T'ai to be ignorant of matters that even Lin Fang enquires into![4]

7   The Master said, Gentlemen never compete. You will say that in archery they do so. But even then they bow and make way for one another when they are going up to the archery-ground, when they are coming down and at the subsequent drinking-bout. Thus even when competing, they still remain gentlemen.

1   Where in several States the ruling families had been ousted by usurpers.
2   To the spirit of the mountain, a thing which the Duke alone had the right to do. The offering is said to have consisted of jade objects.
3   Who was in the service of the Chi family.
4   The mountain must surely know enough of ritual to be aware that no sacrifice but the Duke's could be accepted. The sense is carried on from IV, 4.

（八）

　　子夏问曰：　"'巧笑倩兮，美目盼兮，素以为绚兮。'　何谓也？"子曰：　"绘事后素。"曰：　"礼后乎？"子曰：　"起予者商也，始可与言《诗》已矣。"

（九）

　　子曰：　"夏礼吾能言之，杞不足征也；殷礼吾能言之，宋不足征也：文献不足故也。足，则吾能征之矣。"

（十）

　　子曰：　"禘自既灌而往者，吾不欲观之矣。"

8 Tzu-hsia asked, saying, What is the meaning of

> Oh the sweet smile dimpling,
> The lovely eyes so black and white!
> Plain silk that you would take for coloured stuff.[1]

The Master said, The painting comes after the plain groundwork.[2] Tzu-hsia said, Then ritual comes afterwards?[3] The Master said, Shang[4] it is who bears me up. At last I have someone with whom I can discuss the Songs!

9 The Master said, How can we talk about the ritual of the Hsia? The State of Ch'i[5] supplies no adequate evidence. How can we talk about the ritual of Yin? The State of Sung supplies no adequate evidence. For there is a lack both of documents and of learned men. But for this lack we should be able to obtain evidence from these two States.

10 The Master said, At the Ancestral Sacrifice, as for all that comes after the libation, I had far rather not witness it![6]

1 So dazzling is the contrast that the effect is that of painted stuff rather than of a design in black and white. The first two lines occur in *Song* 86 where however they are not followed by the third line.
2 Confucius reinterprets the third line of verse in the sense 'It is on plain silk that one makes coloured designs', or the like. In scriptural reinterpretation the fact that the new meaning does not fit in with the original context is of no consequence.
3 Can only be built upon Goodness.
4 Familiar names of Tzu-hsia. For a further discussion of this passage, see additional notes.
5 In Honan, where descendants of the Hsia still carried on the sacrifices, Confucius laments that these States had not preserved the documents and rites of their ancestors. The interrogative particles seem to have been accidentally omitted.
6 In interpreting such passages as this we have to be careful not to read them in the light of later and to a large extent Utopian, theoretical books of ritual. Confucius was obviously displeased by the way in which the *Ti* (Ancestor-sacrifice) was carried out in Lu, presumably because it was too closely modelled on Imperial ritual; more than that we cannot say.

（十一）

或问禘之说。子曰：　"不知也。知其说者之于天下也，其如示诸斯乎？"指其掌。

（十二）

祭如在，祭神如神在。子曰：　"吾不祭与，如不祭。"

（十三）

王孙贾问曰：　"与其媚于奥，宁媚于灶，何谓也？"子曰：　"不然。获罪于天，无所祷也。"

（十四）

子曰：　"周监于二代，郁郁乎文哉！吾从周。"

11 Someone asked for an explanation of the Ancestral Sacrifice. The Master said, I do not know. Anyone who knew the explanation could deal with all things under Heaven as easily as I lay this here; and he laid his finger upon the palm of his hand.[1]

12 Of the saying, 'The word "sacrifice" is like the word "present"; one should sacrifice to a spirit as though[2] that spirit was present', the Master said, If I am not present at the sacrifice, it is as though there were no sacrifice.[3]

13 Wang-sun Chia[4] asked about the meaning of the saying,

> Better pay court to the stove
> Than pay court to the Shrine.[5]

The Master said, It is not true. He who has put himself in the wrong with Heaven has no means of expiation left.

14 The Master said, Chou could survey the two preceding dynasties. How great a wealth of culture! And we follow upon Chou.[6]

1 For this anecdote, cf. *Chung Yung*, XIX, 6, and *K'ung Tzu Chia Yü*, 27. (Lun Li).

2 i.e. with the same demeanour and expression. cf. *Li Chi*, XIII, end, 'In general, in sacrifice demeanour and expression should be as though one were in the presence of the person who is being sacrificed to.'

3 i.e. do not worry about 'spirits being present' and the like. What matters is the state of mind of the sacrificer. If he is not heart and soul 'there', the sacrifice is useless. On the purely subjective value of sacrifice, see *Hsün Tzu*, P'ien XIX, end.

4 Commander-in-chief in the State of Wei, mentioned under the year 502 BC in the *Tso Chuan*.

5 This rhymed saying means that it is better to be on good terms with the hearth-god and have a full belly than waste one's food on the Ancestors, who cannot enjoy it. Confucius, who is usually able to reinterpret old maxims in a new, moral sense, finds himself obliged to reject this cynical piece of peasant-lore *in toto*.

6 i.e. we in Lu have all three dynasties, Hsia, Yin, and Chou to look back upon and imitate.

（十五）

子入太庙，每事问。或曰："孰谓鄹人之子知礼乎？入太庙，每事问。"子闻之，曰："是礼也。"

（十六）

子曰："射不主皮，为力不同科，古之道也。"

（十七）

子贡欲去告朔之饩羊。子曰："赐也，尔爱其羊，我爱其礼。"

（十八）

子曰："事君尽礼，人以为谄也。"

（十九）

定公问："君使臣，臣事君，如之何？"孔子对曰："君使臣以礼，臣事君以忠。"

15 When the Master entered the Grand Temple[1] he asked questions about everything there. Someone said, Do not tell me that this son of a villager from Tsou[2] is expert in matters of ritual. When he went to the Grand Temple, he had to ask about everything. The Master hearing of this said, Just so! such is the ritual.[3]

16 The Master said, The saying

> In archery it is not the hide that counts,
> For some men have more strength than others,

is the way of the Ancients.[4]

17 Tzu-kung wanted to do away with the presentation[5] of a sacrificial sheep at the announcement[6] of each new moon. The Master said, Ssu! You grudge sheep, but I grudge ritual.

18 The Master said, Were anyone today to serve his prince according to the full prescriptions of ritual, he would be thought a sycophant.

19 Duke Ting (died 495 BC) asked for a precept concerning a ruler's use of his ministers and a minister's service to his ruler. Master K'ung replied saying, A ruler in employing his ministers should be guided solely by the prescriptions of ritual. Ministers in serving their ruler, solely by devotion to his cause.

1 Erected in honour of the first Duke of Chou.
2 A village with which Confucius's family had been connected.
3 i.e. precisely by doing so I showed my knowledge of ritual; for the asking of such questions is prescribed by ritual. For questions of this sort, see additional notes.
4 i.e. it is not piercing the hide stretched as a target that counts. In this ancient rhymed saying Confucius saw a maxim which metaphorically resumed the whole way of the Ancient Sages, who ruled by Goodness, not by force. For the first of the two lines, cf. *I Li*, Couvreur's translation, p. 173. cf. also *Chou Li*, where *chu p'i* seems merely to mean 'hitting the target'. See additional notes.
5 By the Duke to his State officers. This is the explanation of Liu T'ai-kung (1751–1805). See H.C.C.C. 798.
6 To the Ancestors, who are kept informed of everything that goes on below.

（二十）

子曰：“《关雎》，乐而不淫，哀而不伤。”

（二十一）

哀公问社于宰我。宰我对曰：“夏后氏以松，殷人以柏，周人以栗，曰：使民战栗也。”子闻之，曰：“成事不说，遂事不谏，既往不咎。”

（二十二）

子曰：“管仲之器小哉！”或曰：“管仲俭乎？”曰：“管氏有三归，官事不摄，焉得俭？”“然则管仲知礼乎？”曰：“邦君树塞门，管氏亦树塞门。

20 The Master said, The Ospreys![1] Pleasure not carried to the point
    of debauch; grief not carried to the point of self-injury.

21 Duke Ai asked Tsai Yü[2] about the Holy Ground. Tsai Yü replied,
    The Hsia sovereigns marked theirs with a pine, the men of Yin
    used a cypress, the men of Chou used a chestnut-tree, saying,
    'This will cause the common people to be in fear and trembling.'[3]
    The Master hearing of it said, What is over and done with, one
    does not discuss. What has already taken its course, one does not
    criticise; what already belongs to the past, one does not censure.[4]

22 The Master said, Kuan Chung[5] was in reality a man of very
    narrow capacities. Someone said, Surely he displayed an example
    of frugality? The Master said, Kuan had three lots of wives,[6] his
    State officers performed no double duties. How can he be cited as
    an example of frugality? That may be, the other said; but surely he
    had a great knowledge of ritual? The Master said, Only the ruler
    of a State may build a screen to mask his gate; but Kuan had such

---

1   *The Book of Songs*, No. 87, which begins by describing a lover's grief at
    being separated from his lady and ends by describing their joyful union.
    Confucius sees in it a general guide to conduct, whether in joy or
    affliction. The opening words are: '*Kuan, kuan* cry the ospreys.'
2   A disciple in whom Confucius was much disappointed.
3   Pun on *li* a chestnut-tree and *li* 'to be in awe'.
4   The usual explanation of this passage makes Confucius's comment refer
    to Tsai Yü's pun 'which might lead the Duke to severe measures' in
    dealing with his people (Legge, p. 26). The comment, however, is
    phrased in such a way that it must be taken as referring to the remote
    and not to the immediate past. It is perhaps unfortunate, Confucius
    suggests, that the founders of the Chou dynasty chose a tree with so
    inauspicious a name; but it was ill-bred of Tsai Yü to criticise them in
    conversation with Duke Ai of Lu, who was their direct descendant.
5   Kuan Tzu, seventh century BC, the statesman who built up the power
    of the Ch'i kingdom. Confucius regarded him as having merely
    increased the political prestige of his country without raising its moral
    status.
6   Each consisting of a wife and two 'understudies' (bridesmaids); only a
    feudal lord was entitled to such an establishment.

邦君为两君之好有反坫，管氏亦有反坫。管氏而知礼，孰不知礼！"

（二十三）

子语鲁太师乐，曰：　"乐其可知也。始作，翕如也。从之，纯如也，皦如也，绎如也。以成。"

（二十四）

仪封人请见，曰：　"君子之至于斯者，吾未尝不得见也。"从者见之。出，曰：　"二三子何患于丧乎？天下之无道也久矣，天将以夫子为木铎。"

（二十五）

子谓《韶》，　"尽美矣，又尽善也。"谓《武》，"尽美矣，未尽善也。"

（二十六）

子曰：　"居上不宽，为礼不敬，临丧不哀，吾何以观之哉？"

a screen. Only the ruler of a State, when meeting another such ruler, may use cup-mounds;[1] but Kuan used one. If even Kuan is to be cited as an expert in ritual, who is not an expert in ritual?

23 When talking to the Grand Master[2] of Lu about music, the Master said, Their music[3] in so far as one can find out about it began with a strict unison. Soon the musicians were given more liberty;[4] but the tone remained harmonious, brilliant, consistent, right on till the close.

24 The guardian of the frontier-mound at I[5] asked to be presented to the Master, saying, No gentleman arriving at this frontier has ever yet failed to accord me an interview. The Master's followers presented him. On going out the man said, Sirs, you must not be disheartened by his failure. It is now a very long while[6] since the Way prevailed in the world. I feel sure that Heaven intends to use your Master as a wooden bell.[7]

25 The Master spoke of the Succession Dance[8] as being[9] perfect beauty and at the same time perfect goodness; but of the War Dance as being perfect beauty, but not perfect goodness.

26 The Master said, High office filled by men of narrow views, ritual performed without reverence, the forms of mourning observed without grief – these are things I cannot bear to see!

1 A mound upon which to stand pledge-cups.
2 The *maestro*, music-master, who was always a blind man.
3 The music of the ancients.
4 To improvise.
5 On the borders of the State of Wei.
6 Sages appear at regular intervals. One is now due.
7 A rattle, used to arouse the populace in times of night-danger, and in general by heralds and town-criers; cf. *Li Chi*, Yüeh-ling. (Couvreur's translation, 1, 343).
8 This dance (at any rate according to the later Confucian theory) mimed the peaceful accession of the legendary Emperor Shun; the War Dance mimed the accession by conquest of the Emperor Wu, who overthrew the Yin. See above, II, 23.
9 Or as we should say, 'as embodying'.

里仁第四

（一）

子曰：“里仁为美。择不处仁，焉得知！”

（二）

子曰：“不仁者，不可以久处约，不可以长处乐。仁者安仁，智者利仁。”

（三）

子曰：“唯仁者能好人，能恶人。”

（四）

子曰：“苟志于仁矣，无恶也。”

BOOK FOUR

1 The Master said, It is Goodness that gives to a neighbourhood its beauty.[1] One who is free to choose, yet does not prefer to dwell among the Good – how can he be accorded the name of wise?[2]

2 The Master said, Without Goodness a man

> Cannot for long endure adversity,
> Cannot for long enjoy prosperity.

The Good Man rests content with Goodness; he that is merely wise pursues Goodness in the belief that it pays to do so.

3, 4 Of the adage[3] 'Only a Good Man knows how to like people, knows how to dislike them,' the Master said, He whose heart is in the smallest degree set upon Goodness will dislike no one.

1 cf. *Mencius*, II, A, 7.
2 A justification of the maxim, 'When right does not prevail in a kingdom, then leave it,' and of Confucius's own prolonged travels.
3 cf. *Ta Hsüeh* (The Great Learning), commentary, X, 15. 'Only the Good man is considered capable of loving (*ai*) men, capable of hating them.' In the *Kuo Yü* (ch. 18), however, the saying is quite differently interpreted: 'Only a good man is safe to like and safe to dislike . . . For if you like him, he will not take undue advantage of it; and if you dislike him, he will not resent it.' The words 'The Master said' at the beginning of paragraph 3 should be omitted, and paragraphs 3 and 4 taken together.

（五）

子曰：“富与贵，是人之所欲也，不以其道，得
之不处也。贫与贱，是人之所恶也，不以其道，得之
不去也。君子去仁，恶乎成名？君子无终食之间违仁，
造次必于是，颠沛必于是。”

（六）

子曰：“我未见好仁者，恶不仁者。好仁者，无
以尚之。恶不仁者，其为仁矣，不使不仁者加乎其身。
有能一日用其力于仁矣乎？我未见力不足者。盖有之
矣，我未之见也。”

（七）

子曰：“人之过也，各于其党。观过，斯知仁矣。”

（八）

子曰：“朝闻道，夕死可矣。”

（九）

子曰：“士志于道，而耻恶衣恶食者，未足与议
也。”

5   Wealth and rank are what every man desires; but if they can only be retained to the detriment of the Way he professes, he must relinquish them. Poverty and obscurity are what every man detests; but if they can only be avoided to the detriment of the Way he professes, he must accept them. The gentleman who ever parts company with Goodness does not fulfil that name. Never for a moment[1] does a gentleman quit the way of Goodness. He is never so harried but that he cleaves to this; never so tottering but that he cleaves to this.

6   The Master said, I for my part[2] have never yet seen one who really cared for Goodness, nor one who really abhorred wickedness. One who really cared for Goodness would never let any other consideration come first. One who abhorred wickedness would be so constantly doing Good that wickedness would never have a chance to get at him. Has anyone ever managed to do Good with his whole might even as long as the space of a single day? I think not. Yet I for my part have never seen anyone give up such an attempt because he had not the *strength* to go on. It may well have happened, but I for my part have never seen it.[3]

7   The Master said, Every man's faults belong to a set.[4] If one looks out for faults it is only as a means of recognising Goodness.

8   The Master said, In the morning, hear the Way; in the evening, die content![5]

9   The Master said, A Knight whose heart is set upon the Way, but who is ashamed of wearing shabby clothes and eating coarse food, is not worth calling into counsel.

---

1   Literally, 'for as long as it takes to eat' one bowl of rice. A common impression, simply meaning a very little while.
2   *Wo* as a nominative is more emphatic than *wu*.
3   It is the will not the way that is wanting.
4   i.e. a set of qualities which includes virtues.
5   The well-known saying *Vedi Napoli e poi mori* [See Naples and then die] follows the same pattern. The meaning is, you will have missed nothing.

（十）

　　子曰："君子之于天下也，无适也，无莫也，义之与比。"

（十一）

　　子曰："君子怀德，小人怀土。君子怀刑，小人怀惠。"

（十二）

　　子曰："放于利而行，多怨。"

（十三）

　　子曰："能以礼让为国乎，何有？不能以礼让为国，如礼何？"

（十四）

　　子曰："不患无位，患所以立。不患莫己知，求为可知也。"

10 The Master said, A gentleman in his dealings with the world has neither enmities nor affections;[1] but wherever he sees Right he ranges himself beside it.

11 The Master said, Where gentlemen set their hearts upon moral force (te)[2] the commoners set theirs upon the soil.[3] Where gentlemen think only of punishments, the commoners think only of exemptions.[4]

12 The Master said, Those[5] whose measures are dictated by mere expediency will arouse continual discontent.

13 The Master said, If it is really possible to govern countries by ritual and yielding, there is no more to be said. But if it is not really possible, of what use is ritual?[6]

14 The Master said, He[7] does not mind not being in office; all he minds about is whether he has qualities that entitle him to office. He does not mind failing to get recognition; he is too busy doing the things that entitle him to recognition.

1 Reading uncertain, but general sense quite clear.
2 As opposed to physical compulsion. See additional notes.
3 They *an t'u*, 'are content with the soil', and are prepared to defend it.
4 *Hui* means amnesties, immunities, exemptions, as opposed to what is 'lawful and proper'.
5 The rulers and upper classes in general.
6 The saying can be paraphrased as follows: If I and my followers are right in saying that countries can be governed solely by correct carrying out of ritual and its basic principle of 'giving way to others', there is obviously no case to be made out for any other form of government. If on the other hand we are wrong, then ritual is useless. To say, as people often do, that ritual is all very well so long as it is not used as an instrument of government, is wholly to misunderstand the purpose of ritual.
7 The gentleman. But we might translate 'I do not mind', etc.

（十五）

子曰："参乎，吾道一以贯之！"曾子曰："唯。"子出，门人问曰："何谓也？"曾子曰："夫子之道，忠恕而已矣。"

（十六）

子曰："君子喻于义，小人喻于利。"

（十七）

子曰："见贤思齐焉，见不贤而内自省也。"

（十八）

子曰："事父母，几谏，见志不从，又敬不违，劳而不怨。"

（十九）

子曰："父母在，不远游，游必有方。"

（二十）

子曰："三年无改于父之道，可谓孝矣。"

（二十一）

子曰："父母之年，不可不知也，一则以喜，一则以惧。"

15 The Master said, Shên! My Way has one (thread) that
through it. Master Tsêng said, Yes. When the Master
out, the disciples asked, saying What did he mean? Master Tseng
said, Our Master's Way is simply this: Loyalty, consideration.[1]

16 The Master said, A gentleman takes as much trouble to discover
what is right as lesser men take to discover what will pay.

17 The Master said, In the presence of a good man, think all the
time how you may learn to equal him. In the presence of a bad
man, turn your gaze within![2]

18 The Master said, In serving his father and mother a man may
gently remonstrate with them. But if he sees that he has failed to
change their opinion, he should resume an attitude of deference
and not thwart them; may feel discouraged, but not resentful.

19 The Master said, While father and mother are alive, a good son
does not wander far afield; or if he does so, goes only where he
has said he was going.[3]

20 The Master said, If for the whole three years of mourning a son
manages to carry on the household exactly as in his father's day,
then he is a good son indeed.[4]

21 The Master said, It is always better for a man to know the age of
his parents. In the one case[5] such knowledge will be a comfort to
him; in the other,[6] it will fill him with a salutary dread.

1 Loyalty to superiors; consideration for the feelings of others, 'not doing
to them anything one would not like to have done to oneself', as
defined below, XV, 23. 'Loyalty and Consideration' is one of the Nine
Virtues enumerated by the *I Chou Shu*, 29, I verso. cf. also XV, 2 below.

2 'Within yourself scrutinise yourself'. *êrh* is the second person singular
pronoun, not the conjunction?

3 Particularly in order that if they die he may be able to come back and
perform the rites of mourning.

4 cf. I, 11.

5 If he knows that they are not so old as one might think.

6 If he realises that they are very old.

（二十二）

子曰：“古者言之不出，耻躬之不逮也。”

（二十三）

子曰：“以约失之者鲜矣。”

（二十四）

子曰：“君子欲讷于言而敏于行。”

（二十五）

子曰：“德不孤，必有邻。”

（二十六）

子游曰：“事君数，斯辱矣。朋友数，斯疏矣。”

22 The Master said, In old days a man kept a hold on his words, fearing the disgrace that would ensue should he himself fail to keep pace with them.

23 The Master said, Those who err on the side of strictness are few indeed!

24 The Master said, A gentleman covets the reputation of being slow in word but prompt in deed.[1]

25 The Master said, Moral force (*te*) never dwells in solitude; it will always bring neighbours.[2]

26 Tzu-yu said, In the service of one's prince repeated scolding[3] can only lead to loss of favour; in friendship, it can only lead to estrangement.

---

1 cf. *Tao Te Ching*, ch. 45
2 Whenever one individual or one country substitutes *te* for physical compulsion, other individuals or other countries inevitably follow suit.
3 cf. XII, 23 and additional notes.

公冶长第五

（一）

子谓公冶长："可妻也。虽在缧绁之中，非其罪也。"以其子妻之。

子谓南容："邦有道，不废；邦无道，免于刑戮。"以其兄之子妻之。

（二）

子谓子贱："君子哉若人！鲁无君子者，斯焉取斯。"

（三）

子贡问曰："赐也如何？"子曰："汝，器也。"曰："何器也？"曰："瑚琏也。"

BOOK FIVE

1 The Master said of Kung Yeh Ch'ang, Though he has suffered imprisonment, he is not an unfit person to choose as a husband; for it was not through any fault of his own. He married him to his daughter.

   The Master said of Nan Jung,[1] In a country ruled according to the Way, he would not be overlooked; in a country not ruled according to the Way, he would manage to avoid capital punishment or mutilation. He married him to his elder brother's[2] daughter.

2 Of Tzu-chien[3] he said, A gentleman indeed is such a one as he! If the land of Lu were indeed without gentlemen, how could he have learnt this?

3 Tzu-kung asked saying, What do you think of me? The Master said, You are a vessel.[4] Tzu-kung said, What sort of vessel? The Master said, A sacrificial vase of jade![5]

1 The commentators identify Nan Jung with Nan-kung Kuo, son of Mêng I Tzu, head of the powerful Mêng Family. This is, however, no ground for this identification, nor any reason to suppose that Confucius ever formed so exalted a family connection.

2 According to later tradition Confucius's elder brother was a cripple and for this reason his duties devolved on Confucius.

3 The disciple Fu Tzu-chien, who figures in later legend as model governor of the town of Shan-fu. See additional notes.

4 A man of particular capacities, but lacking the general state of electness known as *Jen* (Goodness).

5 i.e. the highest sort of vessel.

（四）

或曰："雍也，仁而不佞。"子曰："焉用佞。御人以口给，屡憎于人。不知其仁，焉用佞。"

（五）

子使漆雕开仕。对曰："吾斯之未能信。"子说。

（六）

子曰："道不行，乘桴浮于海。从我者其由与？"子路闻之喜。子曰："由也，好勇过我，无所取材。"

（七）

孟武伯问子路仁乎，子曰："不知也。"又问，子曰："由也，千乘之国，可使治其赋也，不知其仁也。""求也何如？"子曰："求也，千室之邑，百乘之家，可使为之宰也，不知其仁也。""赤也何如？"子曰："赤也，束带立于朝，可使与宾客言也，不知

4   Someone said, Jan Yung is Good, but he is a poor talker. The
     Master said, What need has he to be a good talker? Those who
     down others with clap-trap are seldom popular. Whether he is
     Good, I do not know. But I see no need for him to be a good
     talker.

5   The Master gave Ch'i-tiao K'ai leave to take office, but he
     replied, 'I have not yet sufficiently perfected myself in the virtue
     of good faith.' The Master was delighted.

6   The Master said, The Way makes no progress. I shall get upon a
     raft and float out to sea.[1] I am sure Yu would come with me.
     Tzu-lu on hearing of this was in high spirits. The Master said,
     That is Yu indeed! He sets far too much store by feats of physical
     daring. It seems as though I should never get hold of the right
     sort of people.[2]

7   Mêng Wu Po[3] asked whether Tzu-lu was Good. The Master said,
     I do not know. On his repeating the question the Master said, In a
     country of a thousand war-chariots Yu could be trusted to carry
     out the recruiting. But whether he is Good I do not know. 'What
     about Ch'iu?'[4] The Master said, In a city of a thousand families or
     a baronial family with a hundred chariots he might do well as
     Warden. But whether he is Good, I do not know. 'What about
     Ch'ih?'[5] The Master said, Girt with his sash, standing in his place

---

1   What Confucius proposes is, of course, to go and settle among the
     barbarians. cf. III, 5 and IX, 13. A certain idealisation of the 'noble
     savage' is to be found fairly often in early Chinese literature; cf. the
     eulogy of the barbarians put into the mouth of a Chinese whose
     ancestors had settled among them, *Shih Chi* V, and the maxim 'When
     the Emperor no longer functions, learning must be sought among the
     Four Barbarians', north, west, east, and south (*Tso Chuan*, Chao kung
     seventeenth year).
2   Literally, 'get material'. cf. *I Chou Shu* VIII, I verso. Yu (familiar name
     of Tzu-lu) figures in later legend as a converted swashbuckler, who
     constantly shocked Confucius by his pugnacity.
3   See above, II, 6.
4   The disciple Jan Ch'iu.
5   The disciple Kung-hsi Hua.

其仁也。"

（八）

子谓子贡曰："女与回也孰愈？"对曰："赐也何敢望回。回也闻一以知十，赐也闻一以知二。"子曰："弗如也，吾与女弗如也。"

（九）

宰予昼寝。子曰："朽木不可雕也，粪土之墙不可圬也。于予与何诛？"

子曰："始吾于人也，听其言而信其行；今吾于人也，听其言而观其行。于予与改是。"

（十）

子曰："吾未见刚者。"或对曰："申枨。"子曰："枨也欲，焉得刚？"

（十一）

子贡曰："我不欲人之加诸我也，吾亦欲无加诸人。"子曰："赐也，非尔所及也。"

at Court he might well be charged to converse with strangers and guests. But whether he is Good, I do not know.[1]

8 The Master in discussing Tzu-kung said to him, Which do you yourself think is the better, you or Hui?[2] He answered saying, I dare not so much as look at Hui. For Hui has but to hear one part in ten, in order to understand the whole ten. Whereas if I hear one part, I understand no more than two parts. The Master said, Not equal to him – you and I are not equal to him!

9 Tsai Yü[3] used to sleep during the day. The Master said, Rotten wood cannot be carved, nor a wall of dried dung be trowelled.[4] What use is there in my scolding him any more?

   The Master said, There was a time when I merely listened attentively to what people said, and took for granted that they would carry out their words. Now I am obliged not only to give ear to what they say, but also to keep an eye on what they do. It was my dealings with Tsai Yü that brought about the change.

10 The Master said, I have never yet seen a man who was truly steadfast.[5] Someone answered saying, 'Shên Ch'êng'. The Master said, Ch'êng! He is at the mercy of his desires. How can *he* be called steadfast?

11 Tzu-kung said, What I do not want others to do to me, I have no desire to do to others. The Master said, Oh Ssu! You have not quite got to that point yet.

1 Jan Ch'iu is known to history as a faithful henchman of the Lu dictator. Kung-hsi Hua's ambition was to perfect himself in the etiquette of State ceremonies. See XI, 25.

2 See above, II, 9.

3 See III, 21.

4 i.e. patterned with the trowel. To translate 'be plastered' destroys the parallelism.

5 Impervious to outside influences, intimidations, etc.

(十二)

子贡曰："夫子之文章，可得而闻也。夫子之言
性与天道，不可得而闻也。"

(十三)

子路有闻，未之能行，唯恐有闻。

(十四)

子贡问曰："孔文子何以谓之文也?"子曰："敏
而好学，不耻下问，是以谓之文也。"

(十五)

子谓子产："有君子之道四焉：其行己也恭，其
事上也敬，其养民也惠，其使民也义。"

12 Tzu-kung said, Our Master's views concerning culture and the outward insignia[1] of goodness, we are permitted to hear; but about Man's nature[2] and the ways of Heaven[3] he will not tell us anything at all.

13 When Tzu-lu heard any precept and was still trying unsuccessfully to put it into practice, his one fear was that he might hear some fresh precept.

14 Tzu-kung asked saying, Why was K'ung Wên Tzu called Wên (The Cultured)?[4] The Master said, Because he was diligent[5] and so fond of learning that he was not ashamed to pick up knowledge even from his inferiors.

15 Of Tzu-ch'an[6] the Master said that in him were to be found four of the virtues that belong to the Way of the true gentleman. In his private conduct he was courteous, in serving his master he was punctilious, in providing for the needs of the people he gave them even more than their due; in exacting service from the people, he was just.

1 *Chang* (insignia) means literally 'emblems' (usually representations of birds, beasts or plants) figuring on banners or dresses to show the rank of the owner. Hence metaphorically, the outward manifestations of an inner virtue.

2 As it is before it has been embellished with 'culture'.

3 T'ien Tao. The Tao taught by Confucius only concerned human behaviour (the ways of man); he did not expound a corresponding Heavenly Tao, governing the conduct of unseen powers and divinities.

4 i.e. why was he accorded this posthumous title? He was a statesman of the Wei State who died between 484 and 480 BC. He figures in the chronicles as a disloyal and self-seeking minister.

5 There is perhaps a play on *wên* and *min* (diligent); the two words were pronounced very similarly in ancient Chinese.

6 Minister in the Chêng State; died 522 BC.

（十六）

子曰：　"晏平仲善与人交，久而人敬之。"

（十七）

子曰：　"臧文仲居蔡，山节藻棁，何如其知也?"

（十八）

子张问曰：　"令尹子文三仕为令尹，无喜色。三已之，无愠色。旧令尹之政，必以告新令尹。何如?"子曰：　"忠矣。"曰：　"仁矣乎?"曰：　"未知，焉得仁?"

　　"崔子弑齐君，陈文子有马十乘，弃而违之。至于他邦，则曰：　'犹吾大夫崔子也。' 违之。之一邦，

16　The Master said, Yen P'ing Chung is[1] a good example of what one's intercourse with one's fellow men should be. However long he has known anyone he always maintains the same scrupulous courtesy.

17　The Master said, Tsang Wên Chung[2] kept a Ts'ai tortoise[3] in a hall with the hill-pattern on its pillar tops and the duckweed pattern on its king-posts.[4] Of what sort, pray, was his knowledge?[5]

18　Tzu-chang asked saying, The Grand Minister Tzu-wên[6] was appointed to this office on three separate occasions, but did not on any of these three occasions display the least sign of elation. Three times he was deposed; but never showed the least sign of disappointment. Each time, he duly informed his successor concerning the administration of State affairs during his tenure of office. What should you say of him? The Master said, He was certainly faithful to his prince's interests. Tzu-chang said, Would you not call him Good? The Master said, I am not sure. I see nothing in that to merit the title Good.

　　(Tzu-chang said) When Ts'ui Tzu assassinated the sovereign of Ch'i,[7] Ch'ên Wên Tzu[8] who held a fief of ten war chariots gave it up and went away. On arriving in another State, he said, 'I can see they are no better here than our minister Ts'ui Tzu'; and he

1　O: 'was'. The Ch'i minister Yen Tzu, famous for his wise counsels, died in 500 BC.

2　Minister of Lu in the seventh century BC.

3　The country of Ts'ai was famous for its tortoises.

4　Such decoration was proper only to the Emperor's ancestral temple and palace. cf. *I Chou Shu* 48, end. Kuan Tzu (*Li Chi*, Tsa Ch'i, Couvreur's translation, II, 187) is accused of decorating his palace in the same way.

5　i.e. his knowledge of ritual. For a tortoise kept on a special terrace and smeared daily with the blood of four bulls, see *Kuan Tzu*, P'ien 75. Strictly speaking only rulers kept tortoises for use in divination (*Li Chi* X); ministers used the yarrow-stalks. But we find Tsang's grandson still in possession of a Ts'ai tortoise (*Tso Chuan*, Duke Hsiang twenty-third year); so perhaps the family claimed an hereditary privilege.

6　Middle of the seventh century BC.

7　In 548 BC the Duke of Ch'i had seduced his wife.

8　Another Ch'i minister.

则又曰：'犹吾大夫崔子也。' 违之。何如？"子曰：
"清矣。" 曰： "仁矣乎？" 曰： "未知，焉得仁？"

（十九）

季文子三思而后行。子闻之，曰： "再，斯可矣。"

（二十）

子曰： "宁武子，邦有道则知，邦无道则愚。其
知可及也，其愚不可及也。"

（二十一）

子在陈，曰： "归与，归与! 吾党之小子狂简，斐
然成章，不知所以裁之。"

（二十二）

子曰： "伯夷、叔齐，不念旧恶，怨是用希。"

went away. On arriving in the next country, he said, 'I can see they are no better here than our minister Ts'ui Tzu'; and went away. What should you say of him? The Master said, He was certainly scrupulous. Tzu-chang said, Would you not call him Good? The Master said, I am not sure. I see nothing in that to merit the title Good.

19 Chi Wên Tzu[1] used to think thrice before acting. The Master hearing of it said, Twice is quite enough.[2]

20 The Master said, Ning Wu Tzu[3] 'so long as the Way prevailed in his country he showed wisdom; but when the Way no longer prevailed, he showed his folly.'[4] To such wisdom as his we may all attain; but not to such folly!

21 When the Master was in Ch'ên[5] he said, Let us go back, let us go back! The little ones[6] at home are headstrong and careless. They are perfecting themselves in all the showy insignia of culture without any idea how to use them.

22 The Master said, Po I and Shu Ch'i[7] never bore old ills in mind and had but the faintest feelings of rancour.

1 Died 568 BC.
2 Ch'êng Hao (AD 1032-1085) says that if one thinks more than twice, self-interest begins to come into play.
3 A minister of Wei (seventh century BC), famous for his blind devotion to his prince, whose enemies had incarcerated him in a deep dungeon. Here Ning managed to feed his prince through a tube.
4 Such was the judgment of the world.
5 About 492 BC?
6 Disciples.
7 Legendary brothers, almost always bracketed together in this way. The 'old ills' were the misdeeds of the last Yin ruler. When he was attacked by the Chou tribe, the brothers refused to take up arms against their sovereign, despite his great wickedness. Their lack of yüan (rancour) was a classical theme; cf. VII, 14. This was shown by their attitude after each in turn had resigned his rights of accession to the rulership of the small State to which they belonged. Having proposed this act of 'cession' (jang), they carried it out loyally and uncomplainingly.

（二十三）

子曰： "孰谓微生高直?或乞醯焉，气诸其邻而与之。"

（二十四）

子曰： "巧言、令色、足恭，左丘明耻之，丘亦耻之。匿怨而友其人，左丘明耻之，丘亦耻之。"

（二十五）

颜渊、季路侍。子曰： "盍各言尔志?" 子路曰： "愿车马，衣轻裘，与朋友共，敝之而无憾。" 颜渊曰： "愿无伐善，无施劳。" 子路曰： "愿闻子之志。"

23 The Master said, How can we call even Wei-shêng Kao upright? When someone asked him for vinegar he went and begged it from the people next door, and then gave it as though it were his own gift.[1]

24 The Master said, Clever talk, a pretentious manner and a reverence that is only of the feet[2] – Tso Ch'iu Ming[3] was incapable of stooping to them, and I too could never stoop to them. Having to conceal one's indignation and keep on friendly terms with the people against whom one feels it – Tso Ch'iu Ming was incapable of stooping to such conduct, and I too am incapable of stooping to such conduct.[4]

25 Once when Yen Hui and Tzu-lu were waiting upon him the Master said, Suppose each of you were to tell his wish. Tzu-lu said, I should like to have carriages and horses, clothes and fur rugs, share them with my friends and feel no annoyance if they were returned to me the worse for wear. Yen Hui said, I should like never to boast of my good qualities nor make a fuss about the trouble I take on behalf of others. Tzu-lu said, A thing I should like

1 Wei-shêng Kao (see *Chuang Tzu* XXIX, 1, *Chan Kuo Ts'ê*, Yen stories, Pt. 1, *Huai-nan Tzu* XVII, end) is the legendary paragon of truthfulness. Confucius adopts the same formula as the rhyme:

> The Germans in Greek
> Are sadly to seek.
> All except Hermann;
> And Hermann is a German.

How rare, how almost non-existent a quality uprightness must be, Confucius bitterly says, if even into the legend of the most upright of all men there has crept an instance of falsity!

Translators have supposed Wei-shêng Kao to have been some actual contemporary of Confucius, whose conduct the Master was criticising. This misses the whole point.

2 cf. *Ta Tai Li Chi*, 49, where 'foot reverence' is coupled with 'mouth holiness'.

3 See additional notes.

4 And am therefore unfitted for court life, where such behaviour is the sole way to preferment.

子曰：“老者安之，朋友信之，少者怀之。”

（二十六）

子曰：“已矣乎！吾未见能见其过而内自讼者也。”

（二十七）

子曰：“十室之邑，必有忠信如丘者焉，不如丘之好学也。”

is to hear the Master's wish. The Master said, In dealing with the aged, to be of comfort to them; in dealing with friends, to be of good faith with them; in dealing with the young, to cherish them.

26 The Master said, In vain have I looked for a single man capable of seeing his own faults and bringing the charge home against himself.

27 The Master said, In an hamlet of ten houses you may be sure of finding someone quite as loyal and true to his word as I. But I doubt if you would find anyone with such a love of learning.[1]

---

1   i.e. self-improvement in the most general sense. Not book-learning.

雍也第六

（一）

　　子曰：“雍也可使南面。”仲弓问子桑伯子，子
曰：“可也，简。”仲弓曰：“居敬而行简，以临其
民，不亦可乎? 居简而行简，无乃太简乎?”子曰：“雍
之言然。”

（二）

　　哀公问：“弟子孰为好学?”孔子对曰：“有颜回
者好学，不迁怒，不贰过，不幸短命死矣。今也则亡，
未闻好学者也。”

BOOK SIX

1   The Master said, Now Yung,[1] for example. I should not mind
    setting him with his face to the south.[2] Jan Yung then asked
    about Tzu-sang Po-tzu.[3] The Master said, He too would do. He
    is lax.[4] Jan Yung said, I can understand that such a man might do
    as a ruler, provided he were scrupulous in his own conduct and
    lax only in his dealings[5] with the people. But you would admit
    that a man who was lax in his own conduct as well as in
    government would be too lax.[6] The Master said, What Yung
    says is quite true.

2   Duke Ai asked which of the disciples had a love of learning.
    Master K'ung answered him saying, There was Yen Hui. He had
    a great love of learning. He never vented his wrath upon the
    innocent nor let others suffer for his faults. Unfortunately the
    span of life allotted to him by Heaven was short, and he died. At
    present there are none or at any rate I have heard of none who
    are fond of learning.[7]

1   The disciple Jan Yung.
2   Trying him as a ruler.
3   cf. the Tzu-sang of *Chuang Tzu* VI, 11.
4   This is a paradox, *chien* (lax) being generally used in a bad sense.
5   i.e. in the exaction of taxes, corvées, and the like. I punctuate after
    ching, not after *chien*.
6   i.e. too lax to 'set with his face to the south'.
7   cf. XI, 6.

(三)

　　子华使于齐，冉子为其母请粟，子曰："与之釜。"请益，曰："与之庾。"冉子与之粟五秉。子曰："赤之适齐也，乘肥马，衣轻裘。吾闻之也，君子周急不继富。"

　　原思为之宰，与之粟九百，辞。子曰："毋! 以与尔邻里乡党乎?"

(四)

　　子谓仲弓曰："犁牛之子骍且角，虽欲勿用，山川其舍诸?"

(五)

　　子曰："回也，其心三月不违仁，其余则日月至焉而已矣。"

3 When Kung-hsi Hua was sent on a mission to Ch'i, Master Jan asked[1] that Hua's mother might be granted an allowance of grain. The Master said, Give her a cauldron[2] full. Jan said that was not enough. The Master said, Give her a measure.[3] Master Jan gave her five bundles.[4] The Master said, When Ch'ih[5] went to Ch'i he drove sleek horses and was wrapped in light furs. There is a saying, A gentleman helps out the necessitous; he does not make the rich richer still.

When Yüan Ssu was made a governor, he was given an allowance of nine hundred measures of grain, but declined it. The Master said, Surely you could find people who would be glad of it among your neighbours or in your village?

4 The Master said of Jan Yung, If the offspring of a brindled[6] ox is ruddy-coated[7] and has grown its horns, however much people might hesitate to use it,[8] would the hills and streams really reject it?

5 The Master said, Hui is[9] capable of occupying his whole mind for three months on end with no thought but that of Goodness. The others can do so, some for a day, some even for a month; but that is all.[10]

1 i.e. asked the government (the Chi Family), in whose service he was.
2 A merely nominal amount. Confucius disapproved of her being given any at all.
3 A good deal more; but still not a great deal.
4 Ten times (?) more than a measure. Jan entirely disregards Confucius's advice.
5 i.e. Kung-hsi Hua. He ought to have left behind sufficient provision for his mother.
6 i.e. one unsuitable for sacrifice.
7 All over. Only animals of one colour could be used for sacrifice.
8 In sacrificing to the hills and streams. The implication is that Jan Yung was of humble origin. This, says Confucius, ought not to prejudice us against him.
9 There is nothing to indicate whether this was said before or after Yen Hui's premature death.
10 On the strength of sayings such as this, the Taoists claimed Yen Hui as an exponent of *tso-wang* (sitting with blank mind), the Chinese equivalent of yoga.

(六)

季康子问："仲由可使从政也与?"子曰："由也果,于从政乎何有?"曰："赐也可使从政也与?"曰："赐也达,于从政乎何有?"曰："求也可使从政也与?"曰："求也艺,于从政乎何有?"

(七)

季氏使闵子骞为费宰,闵子骞曰："善为我辞焉。如有复我者,则吾必在汶上矣。"

(八)

伯牛有疾,子问之,自牖执其手,曰："亡之,命矣夫! 斯人也而有斯疾也,斯人也而有斯疾也。"

(九)

子曰："贤哉回也! 一箪食,一瓢饮,在陋巷,人不堪其忧,回也不改其乐。贤哉回也!"

6 Chi K'ang-tzu[1] asked whether Tzu-lu was the right sort of person to put into office. The Master said, Yu is efficient. It goes without saying that he is capable of holding office. Chi K'ang-tzu said, How about Tzu-kung? Would he be the right sort of person to put into office? The Master said, He can turn his merits to account.[2] It goes without saying, that he is capable of holding office. Chi K'ang-tzu said, How about Jan Ch'iu? Would he be the right sort of person to put into office? The Master said, He is versatile. It goes without saying that he is capable of holding office.

7 The Chi Family[3] wanted to make Min Tzu-ch'ien governor of Pi.[4] Min Tzu-ch'ien said, Invent a polite excuse for me. If that is not accepted and they try to get at me again, I shall certainly install myself on the far side of the Wên.[5]

8 When Jan Kêng was ill, the Master went to enquire after him, and grasping his hand through the window said, It is all over with him! Heaven has so ordained it – [6] But that such a man should have such an illness! That such a man should have such an illness![7]

9 The Master said, Incomparable indeed was Hui! A handful[8] of rice to eat, a gourdful of water to drink, living in a mean street – others would have found it unendurably depressing, but to Hui's cheerfulness it made no difference at all. Incomparable indeed was Hui![9]

1 Became head of the actual administration of Lu in 492 BC.
2 For *ta*, see additional notes.
3 i.e. the government. He would not serve a usurper.
4 The great stronghold of the Chi Family.
5 i.e. I shall take refuge in the neighbouring land of Ch'i, where I cannot be got at. He was faithful to the legitimate ruler, the Duke of Lu.
6 And we must not repine.
7 Later tradition very naturally explains the passage by saying that Jan Kêng's illness was leprosy. This fits in with the concluding words and also explains why Confucius did not enter the house.
8 Literally, a split bamboo-sectionful.
9 cf. *Mencius*, IV, B, 29.

（十）

冉有曰：“非不说子之道也，力不足也。” 子曰：“力不足者，中道而废。今女画。”

（十一）

子谓子夏曰：“女为君子儒，毋为小人儒。”

（十二）

子游为武城宰，子曰：“女得人焉耳乎?” 曰：有澹台灭明者，行不由径，非公事，未尝至于偃之室也。”

（十三）

子曰：“孟之反不伐，奔而殿，将入门，策其马，曰：‘非敢后也，马不进也。’”

（十四）

子曰：“不有祝鲇之佞，而有宋朝之美，难乎免于今之世矣。”

10 Jan Ch'iu said, It is not that your Way does not commend itself
to me, but that it demands powers I do not possess. The Master
said, He whose strength gives out collapses during the course of
the journey (the Way); but you deliberately draw the line.[1]

11 The Master said to Tzu-hsia, You must practise the *ju*[2] of
gentlemen, not that of the common people.

12 When Tzu-yu was Warden of the castle of Wu, the Master said,
Have you managed to get hold of the right sort of people there?
Tzu-yu said, There is someone called T'an-t'ai Mieh-ming who
'walks on no bypaths'.[3] He has not once come to my house
except on public business.

13 The Master said, Mêng Chih-fan is no boaster. When his people
were routed[4] he was the last to flee; but when they neared the
city-gate, he whipped up his horses, saying, It was not courage
that kept me behind. My horses were slow.

14 The Master said, Without the eloquence of the priest[5] T'o and
the beauty of Prince Ch'ao of Sung it is hard nowadays to get
through.

1   Metaphor of marking boundary-lines of estates or the like.
2   A word of very uncertain meaning. Perhaps 'unwarlikeness'. See
additional notes. The meaning of the saying may be 'The unwarlikeness
of gentlemen means a preference for *te* (moral force), that of inferior
people is mere cowardice.'
    Hu came ultimately to be the general name for followers of the
Confucian Way.
3   i.e. strictly follows our Way. There is probably some further point in
this story that is lost to us owing to our knowing so little about T'an-
t'ai Mieh-ming.
4   At a battle with Ch'i outside the Lu capital in 484 BC. To belittle his
own achievements (the opposite of boasting) is the duty of a gallant
gentleman. So a modern airman who had stayed behind to fight a rear
action might say, 'I was in a funk all the time, but I couldn't get away;
my engine was missing fire.'
5   The *chu* (priest) recited invocations addressed to the ancestors. Both
T'o and Chao flourished about 500 BC.

(十五)

子曰：“谁能出不由户，何莫由斯道也!”

(十六)

子曰：“质胜文则野，文胜质则史，文质彬彬，然后君子。”

(十七)

子曰：“人之生也直，罔之生也幸而免。”

(十八)

子曰：“知之者不如好之者，好之者不如乐之者。”

(十九)

子曰：“中人以上，可以语上也；中人以下，不可以语上也。”

(二十)

樊迟问知。子曰：“务民之义，敬鬼神而远之，可谓知矣。”问仁。曰：“仁者先难而后获，可谓仁矣。”

15 The Master said, Who expects to be able to go out of a house except by the door? How is it then that no one follows this Way of ours?[1]

16 The Master said, When natural substance prevails over ornamentation,[2] you get the boorishness of the rustic. When ornamentation prevails over natural substance, you get the pedantry of the scribe. Only when ornament and substance are duly blended do you get the true gentleman.

17 The Master said, Man's very life is honesty, in that without it he will be lucky indeed if he escapes with his life.[3]

18 The Master said, To prefer it[4] is better than only to know it. To delight in it is better than merely to prefer it.

19 The Master said, To men who have risen at all above the middling sort, one may talk of things higher yet. But to men who are at all below the middling sort it is useless to talk of things that are above them.[5]

20 Fan Ch'ih asked about wisdom.[6] The Master said, He who devotes himself to securing for his subjects what it is right they should have, who by respect for the Spirits keeps them at a distance,[7] may be termed wise. He asked about Goodness. The Master said, Goodness cannot be obtained till what is difficult[8] has been duly done. He who has done this may be called Good.

1 Though it is the obvious and only legitimate way out of all our difficulties.
2 i.e. when nature prevails over culture.
3 I punctuate after *chih*, not after *yeh*.
4 The Way.
5 That belong to a higher stage of learning.
6 i.e. to what rulers the title 'Wise' could be accorded.
7 When the Spirits of hills and streams do not receive their proper share of ritual and sacrifice they do not 'keep their distance', but 'possess' human beings, causing madness, sickness, pestilence, etc.
8 This only becomes intelligible when we refer to XIV, 2, where we see that the 'difficult thing' is to rid oneself of love of mastery, vanity, resentment, and covetousness.

(二十一)

子曰： "知者乐水，仁者乐山。知者动，仁者静。知者乐，仁者寿。"

(二十二)

子曰： "齐一变，至于鲁；鲁一变，至于道。"

(二十三)

子曰： "觚不觚，觚哉，觚哉！"

(二十四)

宰我问曰： "仁者虽告之曰井有仁者焉，其从之也?" 子曰： "何为其然也。君子可逝也，不可陷也；可欺也，不可罔也。"

(二十五)

子曰： "君子博学于文，约之以礼，亦可以弗畔矣夫！"

21 The Master said, The wise man delights in water, the Good man delights in mountains. For the wise move; but the Good stay still. The wise are happy; but the Good, secure.[1]

22 A single change could bring Ch'i to the level of Lu; and a single change would bring Lu to the Way.

23 The Master said, A horn-gourd that is neither horn nor gourd! A pretty horn-gourd indeed, a pretty horn-gourd indeed.[2]

24 Tsai Yü asked saying, I take it a Good Man, even if he were told that another Good Man were at the bottom of a well, would go to join him? The Master said, Why should you think so? 'A gentleman can be broken, but cannot be dented;[3] may be deceived, but cannot be led astray.'[4]

24 (Paraphrased). Tsai Yü half playfully asked whether, since the Good always go to where other Good Men are, a Good Man would leap into a well on hearing that there was another Good Man at the bottom of it. Confucius, responding in the same playful spirit, quotes a maxim about the true gentleman, solely for the sake of the reference in it to *hsien*, which means 'throw down' into a pit or well, but also has the sense 'to pit', 'to dent'.

25 The Master said, A gentleman who is widely versed in letters and at the same time knows how to submit his learning to the restraints of ritual is not likely, I think, to go far wrong.

1 For the origin of this saying, which has here taken on a form distorted by quietist influences, see additional note.

2 A particular sort of bronze goblet was called *ku*, which is written 'horn' beside 'gourd', though the object in question is not shaped like a gourd and is not a drinking-horn. The saying is, of course, a metaphorical way of lamenting over the political state of China, 'ruled over' by an Emperor who had no temporal power and local sovereigns whose rights had been usurped by their ministers.

3 cf. *Shuo Yüan*, XVII: The gentleman (like jade) can be broken, but not bent.

4 i.e. deceived as to facts; but cannot be enticed into wrong conduct. cf. *Mencius*, V, A, 2

（二十六）

　　子见南子，子路不说，夫子矢之曰：　"予所否者，天厌之，天厌之！"

（二十七）

　　子曰：　"中庸之为德也，其至矣乎！民鲜久矣。"

（二十八）

　　子贡曰：　"如有博施于民而能济众，何如？可谓仁乎？"　子曰：　"何事于仁，必也圣乎，尧舜其犹病诸！夫仁者，己欲立而立人，己欲达而达人。能近取譬，可谓仁之方也已。"

26 When the Master went to see Nan-tzu,[1] Tzu-lu was not pleased.
Whereupon the Master made a solemn declaration[2] concerning
his visit, saying, Whatsoever I have done amiss, may Heaven
avert it, may Heaven avert it!

27 The Master said, How transcendent is the moral power of the
Middle Use![3] That it is but rarely found among the common
people is a fact long admitted.[4]

28 Tzu-kung said, If a ruler not only conferred wide benefits upon
the common people, but also compassed the salvation of the
whole State, what would you say of him? Surely, you would call
him Good? The Master said, It would no longer be a matter of
'Good'. He would without doubt be a Divine Sage. Even Yao
and Shun could hardly criticise him.[5] As for Goodness – you
yourself desire rank and standing; then help others to get rank
and standing. You want to turn your own merits to account;
then help others to turn theirs to account – in fact, the ability to
take one's own feelings as a guide – that is the sort of thing that
lies in the direction of Goodness.[6]

1 The wicked concubine of Duke Ling of Wei.
2 See additional notes.
3 Confucius's Way was essentially one of moderation: 'to exceed is as
   bad as to fall short'. See additional notes.
4 *Chiu i* constantly has an idiomatic sense of this sort, and does not mean
   simply 'a long while'. cf. *Doctrine of the Mean*, III.
5 cf. XIV, 45, and *Han Shih Wai Chuan*, VII, 9.
6 For *fang*, 'direction', cf. XI, 25.

述而第七

（一）

子曰：“述而不作，信而好古，窃比于我老彭。”

（二）

子曰：“默而识之，学而不厌，诲人不倦，何有于我哉！”

（三）

子曰：“德之不修，学之不讲，闻义不能从，不善不能改，是吾忧也。”

（四）

子之燕居，申申如也，夭夭如也。

（五）

子曰：“甚矣吾衰也！久矣吾不复梦见周公。”

BOOK SEVEN

1, 2, 3 The Master said, I have 'transmitted what was taught to me
without making up anything of my own'.[1] I have been faithful to
and loved the Ancients. In these respects, I make bold to think,
not even our old P'êng[2] can have excelled me. The Master said,
I have listened in silence and noted what was said, I have never
grown tired of learning nor wearied of teaching others what I
have learnt. These at least are merits which I can confidently
claim.[3] The Master said, The thought that 'I have left my moral
power (*te*) untended, my learning unperfected, that I have heard
of righteous men, but been unable to go to them; have heard of
evil men, but been unable to reform them'[4] – it is these thoughts
that disquiet me.

4   In his leisure hours the Master's manner was very free-and-easy,
and his expression alert and cheerful.

5   The Master said, How utterly have things gone to the bad with
me! It is long now indeed since I dreamed that I saw the Duke of
Chou.

1   cf. *Mo Tzu*, P'ien 46. 'A gentleman does not make anything up; he
merely transmits.'
2   The Chinese Nestor. It is the special business of old men to transmit
traditions.
3   For the idiom *ho yu*, 'there is no further trouble about', see above, IV, 13.
4   The passage in inverted commas consists of two rhymed couplets, and
is probably traditional.

(六)

子曰： "志于道，据于德，依于仁，游于艺。"

(七)

子曰： "自行束脩以上，吾未尝无诲焉。"

(八)

子曰： "不愤不启。不悱不发。举一隅，不以三隅反，则吾不复也。"

(九)

子食于有丧者之侧，未尝饱也。子于是日哭则不歌。

(十)

子谓颜渊曰： "用之则行，舍之则藏，唯我与尔有是夫！"子路曰： "子行三军则谁与？"子曰： "暴虎冯河，死而无悔者，吾不与也。必也，临事而惧，好谋而成者也。"

6 The Master said, Set your heart upon the Way, support yourself by its power, lean upon Goodness, seek distraction in the arts.[1]

7 The Master said, From the very poorest upwards – beginning even with the man who could bring no better present than a bundle of dried flesh[2] – none has ever come to me without receiving instruction.

8 The Master said, Only one who bursts with eagerness do I instruct; only one who bubbles with excitement, do I enlighten. If I hold up one corner and a man cannot come back to me with the other three,[3] I do not continue the lesson.

9 If at a meal the Master found himself seated next to someone who was in mourning, he did not eat his fill. When he had wailed at a funeral, during the rest of the day he did not sing.[4]

10 The Master said to Yen Hui, The maxim

> When wanted, then go;
> When set aside; then hide.

is one that you and I could certainly fulfil. Tzu-lu said, Supposing you had command of the Three Hosts,[5] whom would you take to help you? The Master said, The man who was ready to 'beard a tiger or rush a river'[6] without caring whether he lived or died – that sort of man I should not take. I should certainly take someone who approached difficulties with due caution and who preferred to succeed by strategy.

---

1 Music, archery and the like.
2 See additional notes.
3 Metaphor from laying out of field-plots?
4 Both of these are common ritual prescriptions. cf. *Li Chi* III, fol. 6 and I, fol. 6.
5 i.e. the whole army.
6 cf. *The Book of Songs*, No. 295, verse 6. The reply is clearly intended as a snub to the impulsive Tzu-lu. The song is one which I omit in my translation.

（十一）

子曰："富而可求也，虽执鞭之士，吾亦为之。如不可求，从吾所好。"

（十二）

子之所慎，齐、战、疾。

（十三）

子在齐闻《韶》，三月不知肉味，曰："不图为乐之至于斯也。"

（十四）

冉有曰："夫子为卫君乎?"子贡曰："诺，吾将问之。"入，曰："伯夷、叔齐何人也?"子曰："古人贤人也。"曰："怨乎?"曰："求仁而得仁，又何怨乎?"出，曰："夫子不为也。"

11 The Master said, If any means of escaping poverty presented itself
    that did not involve doing wrong, I would adopt it, even though
    my employment were only that of the gentleman who holds the
    whip.[1] But so long as it is a question of illegitimate means, I shall
    continue to pursue the quests that I love.[2]

12 The rites to which the Master gave the greatest attention were
    those connected with purification before sacrifice, with war and
    with sickness.[3]

13 When he was in Ch'i the Master heard the Succession,[4] and for
    three months did not know the taste of meat.[5] He said I did not
    picture to myself that any music existed which could reach such
    perfection as this.[6]

14 Jan Ch'iu said, Is our Master on the side of the Prince of Wei?[7]
    Tzu-kung said, Yes, I must ask him about that. He went in and
    said, What sort of people were Po I and Shu Ch'i?[8] The Master
    said, They were good men who lived in the days of old. Tzu-
    kung said, Did they repine? The Master said, They sought
    Goodness and got Goodness. Why should they repine? On
    coming out Tzu-kung said, Our Master is not on his side.

1   i.e. the most menial. 'Gentleman', *shih*, in such contexts is used with
    a slightly ironical intention, as one might say in French 'le monsieur
    qui . . . ' cf. *Chuang Tzu* XV, 1.
2   The study of the Ancients.
3   A special sacrifice was held before the departure of military expeditions,
    and the sacrificial meat was distributed among the soldiers. The
    populace flocked to the Ancestral Shrines, wailing to the Ancestors for
    assistance. Sickness was exorcised by sacrifices to hills and streams.
4   See III, 25.
5   i.e. did not notice what he was eating.
6   The older commentators take 'this' to mean the land of Ch'i, i.e. 'I did
    not expect to find such music here in Ch'i.' This may be right.
7   When Duke Ling died in the summer of 493 BC the throne passed to
    his grandson, his son having previously abdicated his rights to the
    accession. Soon, however, the son went back on his word and
    attempted to oust the grandson from the throne.
8   See above, V, 22. The contrast is between Po I and Shu Ch'i on the
    one hand (they are always spoken of as though they were to all intents

(十五)

子曰：“饭疏食，饮水，曲肱而枕之，乐亦在其中矣。不义而富且贵，于我如浮云。”

(十六)

子曰：“加我数年，五十以学《易》，可以无大过矣。”

(十七)

子所雅言，《诗》、《书》、执礼，皆雅言也。

(十八)

叶公问孔子于子路，子路不对。子曰：“女奚不曰：其为人也，发愤忘食，乐以忘忧，不知老之将至

15 The Master said, He who seeks only coarse food to eat, water to drink and a bent arm for pillow, will without looking for it find happiness to boot.[1] Any thought of accepting wealth and rank by means that I know to be wrong is as remote from me as the clouds that float above.

16 The Master said, Give me a few more years, so that I may have spent a whole fifty in study,[2] and I believe that after all I should be fairly free from error.

17 The occasions upon which the Master used correct pronunciation[3] were when reciting the *Songs* or the *Books* and when practising ritual acts. At all such times he used the correct pronunciation.

18 The 'Duke of Shê'[4] asked Tzu-lu about Master K'ung (Confucius). Tzu-lu did not reply. The Master said, Why did you not say 'This is the character of the man: so intent upon enlightening the eager that he forgets his hunger, and so happy in doing so, that he

---

and purposes a single person) and Duke Ling's son on the other. The two 'good men of old' harboured no rancour after their act of cession; whereas Ling's son became discontented with his lot. Tzu-kung sounds Confucius indirectly upon his attitude, because the Master was at this time living in Wei and would have been loath to make an open pronouncement on the question.

1 For the idiom, see II, 18.

2 In common with most scholars, I follow the Lu version here. The Ku version introduces a reference to the *Book of Changes*. But there is no reason to suppose that the *Changes* had in Confucius's time been philosophised, or that he regarded it as anything but a book of divination.

3 Whereas in daily life he used the Lu dialect. Similarly the Swiss, for example, use their own dialect in daily life, but Hochdeutsch in church services or in reciting a poem by Schiller. cf. *Hsün Tzu*, P'ien 4, A man of Yüeh is at ease in Yüeh speech, a man of Ch'u in Ch'u speech. They are gentlemen, in the 'correct pronunciation', *ya*, the same term as is used here. See further, additional notes.

4 An adventurer, known originally as Shên Chu-liang; first mentioned in 523 BC and still alive in 475. The title 'Duke of Shê' was one which he had invented for himself.

云尔。"

(十九)

子曰："我非生而知之者，好古，敏以求之者也。"

(二十)

子不语怪、力、乱、神。

(二十一)

子曰："三人行，必有我师焉。择其善者而从之，其不善者而改之。"

(二十二)

子曰："天生德于予，桓魋其如予何?"

(二十三)

子曰："二三子以我为隐乎?吾无隐乎尔。吾无行而不与二三子者，是丘也。"

(二十四)

子以四教：文、行、忠、信。

forgets the bitterness of his lot and does not realise tha[...]
at hand.[1] That is what he is.'

19 The Master said, I for my part[2] am not one of those who have innate knowledge. I am simply one who loves the past and who is diligent in investigating it.

20 The Master never talked of prodigies, feats of strength, disorders[3] or spirits.

21 The Master said, Even when walking in a party of no more than three I can always be certain of learning from those I am with. There will be good qualities that I can select for imitation and bad ones that will teach me what requires correction in myself.

22 The Master said, Heaven begat the power (te) that is in me. What have I to fear from such a one as Huan T'ui?[4]

23 The Master said, My friends, I know you think that there is something I am keeping from you. There is nothing at all that I keep from you. I take no steps about which I do not consult you, my friends. Were it otherwise, I should not be Ch'iu.[5]

24 The Master took four subjects for his teaching: culture, conduct of affairs, loyalty to superiors and the keeping of promises.

1 According to the traditional chronology Confucius was sixty-two at the time when this was said.
2 *Wo*, emphatic as opposed to the simple nominative *wu*. cf. *Hu Shih Wên Ts'un*, Vol. II, p. 13. cf. IV, 6 and note.
3 Disorders of nature; such as snow in summer, owls hooting by day, or the like.
4 Minister of War in Sung. cf. *Tso Chuan*, Duke Ai fourteenth year.
5 Familiar name of Confucius. There is no evidence that Confucius is here disclaiming the possession of an esoteric doctrine. The wording (*hsing*: steps, *démarches*) suggests that practical steps (with a view to office, patronage or the like) are all that is intended.

(二十五)

　　子曰：“圣人，吾不得而见之矣，得见君子者，斯可矣。”子曰：“善人，吾不得而见之矣，得见有恒者，斯可矣。亡而为有，虚而为盈，约而为泰，难乎有恒矣。”

(二十六)

　　不钓而不纲，弋不射宿。

(二十七)

　　子曰：“盖有不知而作之者，我无是也。多闻，择其善者而从之，多见而识之，知之次也。”

(二十八)

　　互乡难与言。童子见，门人惑。子曰：“与其进也，不与其退也，唯何甚?人洁己以进，与其洁也，不保其往也。”

25 The Master said, A Divine Sage I cannot hope ever to meet; the most I can hope for is to meet a true gentleman. The Master said, A faultless man I cannot hope ever to meet; the most I can hope for is to meet a man of fixed principles. Yet where all around I see Nothing pretending to be Something,[1] Emptiness pretending to be Fullness, Penury pretending to be Affluence, even a man of fixed principles will be none too easy to find.

26 The Master fished with a line but not with a net; when fowling he did not aim at a roosting bird.[2]

27 The Master said, There may well be those who can do without knowledge; but I for my part am certainly not one of them. To hear much, pick out what is good and follow it, to see much and take due note of it,[3] is the lower[4] of the two kinds of knowledge.

28 At Hu village[5] the people were difficult to talk to.[6] But an uncapped[7] boy presented himself for an interview. The disciples were in two minds about showing him in. But the Master said, In sanctioning his entry here I am sanctioning nothing he may do when he retires. We must not be too particular. If anyone purifies[8] himself in order to come to us, let us accept this purification. We are not responsible for what he does when he goes away.

1 An impotent cipher pretending to be a Duke, powerless tools of adventurers such as Yang Huo pretending to be Ministers.

2 For 'fowling', see The Book of Songs, p. 36.

3 As I do.

4 The higher being innate knowledge, which Confucius disclaims above, VII, 19. He thus (ironically) places himself at two removes from the hypothetical people who can dispense with knowledge, the three stages being, (1) those who do not need knowledge; (2) those who have innate knowledge; (3) those who accumulate it by hard work.

5 Unknown. Probably one of the places Confucius passed through during his travels.

6 About the Way. cf. XV, 7.

7 The 'capping' of boys marked their initiation into manhood.

8 A suppliant of any kind (whether asking a Master for teaching or Heaven for good crops) purifies himself by fasting and abstinence in

(二十九)

子曰: "仁远乎哉? 我欲仁, 斯仁至矣。"

(三十)

陈司败问昭公知礼乎, 孔子对曰: "知礼。" 孔子退, 揖巫马期而进之, 曰: "吾闻君子不党, 君子亦党乎? 君娶于吴为同姓, 谓之吴孟子。君而知礼, 孰不知礼?" 巫马期以告。子曰: "丘也幸, 苟有过, 人必知之。"

(三十一)

子与人歌而善, 必使反之, 而后和之。

(三十二)

子曰: "文莫, 吾犹人也。躬行君子, 则吾未之有得。"

(三十三)

子曰: "若圣与仁, 则吾岂敢?抑为之不厌, 诲人

29 The Master said, Is Goodness indeed so far away? If we really wanted Goodness, we should find that it was at our very side.

30 The Minister of Crime in Ch'ên asked whether Duke Chao of Lu knew the rites. Master K'ung said, He knew the rites. When Master K'ung had withdrawn, the Minister motioned Wu-ma Ch'i[1] to come forward and said, I have heard the saying 'A gentleman is never partial.' But it seems that some gentlemen are very partial indeed. His Highness[2] married into the royal family of Wu who belong to the same clan as himself, calling her Wu Mêng Tzu.[3] If his Highness knew the rites, who does not know the rites? Wu-ma Ch'i repeated this to the Master, who said, I am a fortunate man. If by any chance I make a mistake, people are certain to hear of it![4]

31 When in the Master's presence anyone sang a song that he liked, he did not join in at once, but asked for it to be repeated and then joined in.

32 The Master said, As far as taking trouble goes, I do not think I compare badly with other people. But as regards carrying out the duties of a gentleman in actual life, I have never yet had a chance to show what I could do.

33 The Master said, As to being a Divine Sage or even a Good Man, far be it from me to make any such claim. As for unwearying effort to learn and unflagging patience in teaching others,[5] those

---

order to enhance the power of his prayer. For abstinence before entertaining a teacher, cf. *Kuan Tzu*, P'ien 19, where the purification consists in washing in water from a new well, making a burnt offering, and ten days' abstinence and fasting.

1 Later regarded as a disciple of Confucius.

2 Duke Chao, reigned from 541 to 510 BC.

3 He broke the rule of exogamy and hoped to pass this off by speaking of her in a way that might lead people to think she belonged to another clan, the Tzu.

4 This is, of course, ironical. It would have been improper for Confucius to criticise his own late sovereign.

5 cf. *Mencius*, II, A, 2.

不倦，则可谓云尔已矣。"公西华曰：　"正唯弟子不能学也。"

(三十四)

子疾病，子路请祷。子曰：　"有诸?"子路对曰："有之。《诔》曰：'祷尔于上下神祇。'"子曰："丘之祷久矣。"

(三十五)

子曰：　"奢则不逊，俭则固，与其不逊也，宁固。"

(三十六)

子曰：　"君子坦荡荡，小人长戚戚。"

(三十七)

子温而厉，威而不猛，恭而安。

are merits that I do not hesitate to claim. Kung-hsi Hua said, The trouble is that we disciples cannot learn!

34 When the Master was very ill, Tzu-lu asked leave to perform the Rite of Expiation. The Master said, Is there such a thing?[1] Tzu-lu answered saying, There is. In one of the Dirges it says, 'We performed rites of expiation for you, calling upon the sky-spirits above and the earth-spirits below.' The Master said, My expiation began long ago![2]

35 The Master said, Just as lavishness leads easily to presumption, so does frugality to meanness. But meanness is a far less serious fault than presumption.[3]

36 The Master said, A true gentleman is calm and at ease; the Small Man is fretful and ill at ease.

37 The Master's manner was affable yet firm, commanding but not harsh, polite but easy.

1 i.e. is there any ancient authority for such a rite?
2 What justifies me in the eyes of Heaven is the life I have led. There is no need for any rite now. In a fragment of one of the lost books of *Chuang Tzu* there is a parallel story in which Tzu-lu wants to take the omens about Confucius's chance of recovery, and Confucius says 'My omen-taking was done long ago!' See *T'ai P'ing Yü Lan* 849, fol. I verso. The reference was kindly sent to me by Dr Gustav Haloun.
3 cf. III, 4. The lavishness of the Chi Family became presumption when it led them to have eight rows of dancers (III, 1) and thereby infringe upon a ducal prerogative.

泰伯第八

(一)

子曰： "泰伯，其可谓至德也已矣！三以天下让，民无得而称焉。"

(二)

子曰： "恭而无礼则劳，慎而无礼则葸，勇而无礼则乱，直而无礼则绞。君子笃于亲，则民兴于仁。故旧不遗，则民不偷。"

BOOK EIGHT

1 The Master said, Of T'ai Po[1] it may indeed be said that he attained to the very highest pitch of moral power. No less than three times he renounced the sovereignty of all things under Heaven, without the people getting a chance to praise him for it.

2 The Master said, Courtesy not bounded by the prescriptions of ritual becomes tiresome. Caution not bounded by the prescriptions of ritual becomes timidity, daring becomes turbulence, inflexibility becomes harshness.[2]

The Master said,[3] When gentlemen deal generously with their own kin, the common people are incited to Goodness. When old dependents are not discarded, the common people will not be fickle.

---

1 T'ai Po was the eldest son of King Tan, legendary ancestor of the Chou sovereigns. He renounced the Throne in favour of his youngest brother. *Jang* (renunciation) is the virtue that engenders the greatest quantity of *te* (moral power). No renunciation can be greater than to renounce 'the sovereignty of all things under Heaven'. Moreover, a *yin te* (secret accretion of 'power) is always more redoubtable than an open one. The secrecy seems to have been achieved by giving it out that T'ai Po's flight to the lands of Wu and Yüeh was undertaken in order to collect medicines for Old King Tan, who was ill. (Chêng Hsüan makes a rather forced effort to enumerate three separate occasions upon which T'ai Po renounced his claims.)

2 Compare XVII, 8.

3 The Pelliot MS. supplies these words, which have dropped out of the current version.

（三）

　　曾子有疾，召门弟子曰："启予足，启予手。《诗》云：'战战兢兢，如临深渊，如履薄冰。'而今而后，吾知免夫，小子！"

（四）

　　曾子有疾，孟敬子问之。曾子言曰："鸟之将死，其鸣也哀；人之将死，其言也善。君子所贵道者三；动容貌，斯远暴慢矣；正颜色，斯近信矣；出辞气，斯远鄙倍矣。笾豆之事，则有司存。"

（五）

　　曾子曰："以能问于不能，以多问于寡，有若无，实若虚，犯而不校。昔者吾友尝从事于斯矣。"

3 When Master Tsêng was ill he summoned his disciples and said,
Free my feet, free my hands. The *Song* says:

> In fear and trembling,
> With caution and care,
> As though on the brink of a chasm,
> As though treading thin ice.

But I feel now that whatever may betide I have got through
safely, my little ones.[1]

4 When Master Tsêng was ill, Mêng Ching Tzu[2] came to see him.
Master Tsêng spoke to him saying, When a bird is about to die
its song touches the heart.[3] When a man is about to die, his
words are of note. There are three things that a gentleman, in
following the Way, places above all the rest: from every attitude,
every gesture that he employs he must remove all trace of
violence or arrogance; every look that he composes in his face
must betoken good faith; from every word that he utters, from
every intonation, he must remove all trace of coarseness or
impropriety. As to the ordering of ritual vessels and the like, there
are those whose business it is to attend to such matters.

5 Master Tsêng said, Clever, yet not ashamed to consult those less
clever than himself; widely gifted, yet not ashamed to consult
those with few gifts; having, yet seeming not to have; full, yet
seeming empty; offended against, yet never contesting – long ago
I had a friend[4] whose ways were such as this.

1 While a man was dying four people held his hands and feet, 'one for
each limb' (*Li Chi*, XXII). After death, the hands and feet were freed (*Li
I Chih*, supplement to the *Hou Han Shu*, Part III, fol. 1). Tsêng says that
he has got through safely, his moral course is run; there is no need to
hold his hands and feet, which was done 'in case the dying man should
in his death-struggle get into some "non-ritual" attitude'. He interprets
the *Song* 295 as describing the heavy responsibilities of the man who has
'taken Goodness for his load'; see below, VIII, 7. For the anthropological
connotations of 'freeing hands and feet', see additional notes.

2 Son of Mêng Wu Po (see II, 6). He appears to have been still alive in
430 BC.

3 cf. our belief concerning 'swan-songs'.

4 It has been suggested that the friend in question was Yen Hui.

(六)

曾子曰：“可以托六尺之孤，可以寄百里之命，临大节而不可夺也，君子人与？君子人也。”

(七)

曾子曰：“士不可以不弘毅，任重而道远。仁以为己任，不亦重乎？死而后已，不亦远乎？”

(八)

子曰：“兴于《诗》，立于礼，成于乐。”

(九)

子曰：“民可使由之，不可使知之。”

(十)

子曰：“好勇疾贫，乱也。人而不仁，疾之已甚，乱也。”

(十一)

子曰：“如有周公之才之美，使骄且吝，其余不足观也已。”

(十二)

子曰：“三年学，不至于谷，不易得也。”

6 Master Tsêng said, The man to whom one could with equal confidence entrust an orphan not yet fully grown[1] or the sovereignty of a whole State,[2] whom the advent of no emergency however great could upset – would such a one be a true gentleman? He I think would be a true gentleman indeed.

7 Master Tsêng said, The true Knight of the Way must perforce be both broad-shouldered and stout of heart; his burden is heavy and he has far to go. For Goodness is the burden he has taken upon himself; and must we not grant that it is a heavy one to bear? Only with death does his journey end; then must we not grant that he has far to go?

8 The Master said, Let a man be first incited by the *Songs*, then given a firm footing by the study of ritual, and finally perfected by music.

9 The Master said, The common people can be made to follow it;[3] they cannot be made to understand it.

10 The Master said, One who is by nature daring and is suffering from poverty will not long be law-abiding. Indeed, any men, save those that are truly Good, if their sufferings are very great, will be likely to rebel.[4]

11 The Master said, If a man has gifts as wonderful as those of the Duke of Chou, yet is arrogant and mean, all the rest is of no account.

12 The Master said:

> One who will study for three years
> Without thought of reward[5]
> Would be hard indeed to find.

---

1 Literally, an orphan of six feet (i.e. four of our feet).
2 Literally, the command of a hundred leagues.
3 i.e. the Way.
4 Official interpretation, 'Men who are not truly Good, if you criticise them too severely, are likely to rebel.'
5 i.e. of obtaining a paid appointment.

（十三）

子曰：　"笃信好学，守死善道，危邦不入，乱邦不居。天下有道则见，无道则隐。邦有道，贫且贱焉，耻也；邦无道，富且贵焉，耻也。"

（十四）

子曰：　"不在其位，不谋其政。"

（十五）

子曰：　"师挚之始，《关雎》之乱，洋洋乎盈耳哉！"

（十六）

子曰：　"狂而不直，侗而不愿，悾悾而不信，吾不知之矣。"

（十七）

子曰：　"学如不及，犹恐失之。"

（十八）

子曰：　"巍巍乎！舜禹之有天下也，而不与焉。"

（十九）

子曰：　"大哉！尧之为君也。巍巍乎，唯天为大，唯尧则之。荡荡乎，民无能名焉。巍巍乎，其有成功

13 The Master said, Be of unwavering good faith, love learning, if attacked[1] be ready to die for the good Way. Do not enter a State that pursues dangerous courses, nor stay in one where the people have rebelled. When the Way prevails under Heaven, then show yourself; when it does not prevail, then hide. When the Way prevails in your own land, count it a disgrace to be needy and obscure; when the Way does not prevail in your land, then count it a disgrace to be rich and honoured.

14 The Master said, He who holds no rank in a State does not discuss its policies.

15 The Master said, When Chih the Chief Musician led the climax of the *Ospreys*,[2] what a grand flood of sound filled one's ears!

16 The Master said, Impetuous, but tricky! Ingenuous, but dishonest! Simple-minded, but capable of breaking promises![3] To such men I can give no recognition.

17 The Master said, Learn as if you were following someone whom you could not catch up, as though it were someone you were frightened of losing.

18 The Master said, Sublime were Shun and Yü! All that is under Heaven was theirs, yet they remained aloof from it.

19 The Master said, Greatest, as lord and ruler, was Yao.[4] Sublime, indeed, was he. 'There is no greatness like the greatness of Heaven', yet Yao could copy it. So boundless was it[5] that the people could find no name for it;[6] yet sublime were his achievements, dazzling the insignia of his culture!

1 Literally, 'on the defensive'.
2 See III, 20. For Chih, see XVIII, 9.
3 In old days (see XVII, 16) people at any rate had the merits of their faults.
4 cf. *Mencius*, III, a, 4.
5 i.e. Yao's *te*.
6 So that it remained a *yin te* (secret prestige). cf. above, VIII, 1.

也。焕乎，其有文章。"

(二十)

　　舜有臣五人而天下治。武王曰："予有乱臣十人。"
孔子曰："才难，不其然乎？唐虞之际，于斯为盛。有妇
人焉，九人而已。三分天下有其二，以服事殷。周德
其可谓至德也已矣。"

(二十一)

　　子曰："禹，吾无间然矣。菲饮食而致孝乎鬼神，
恶衣服而致美乎黻冕，卑宫室而尽力乎沟洫。禹，吾
无间然矣。"

20 Shun had five ministers and all that is under Heaven was well ruled. King Wu[1] said, I have ten[2] ministers. Master K'ung said, True indeed is the saying that 'the right material is hard to find'; for the turn of the T'ang and Yü dynasties[3] was the time most famous for this.[4] (As for King Wu),[5] there was a woman among his ten, so that in reality there were only nine men. Yet of all that is under Heaven he held two parts in three, using them in submissive service to the dynasty of Yin.[6] The moral power (*te*) of Chou may, indeed, be called an absolutely perfect moral power!

21 The Master said, In Yü I can find no semblance of a flaw. Abstemious in his own food and drink, he displayed the utmost devotion in his offerings to spirits and divinities.[7] Content with the plainest clothes for common wear, he saw to it that his sacrificial apron and ceremonial head-dress were of the utmost magnificence. His place of habitation was of the humblest, and all his energy went into draining and ditching. In him I can find no semblance of a flaw.

1 The Warrior King, founder of the Chou dynasty.
2 His mother, and his nine brothers? See additional notes.
3 i.e. the accession of Shun.
4 i.e. for 'the right material', for an abundance of good ministers. Yet even then there were only five.
5 Some such words have dropped out of the text.
6 And by this act of cession (*jang*) building up the *te* required for his subsequent campaign. For the whole paragraph, see additional notes.
7 To ancestors, and spirits of hill, stream, etc.

子罕第九

（一）

子罕言利，与命，与仁。

（二）

达巷党人曰：　"大哉孔子！博学而无所成名。" 子闻之，谓门弟子曰：　"吾何执？执御乎，执射乎？吾执御矣。"

（三）

子曰：　"麻冕，礼也；今也纯，俭，吾从众。拜下，礼也；今拜乎上，泰也，虽违众，吾从下。"

（四）

子绝四：毋意，毋必，毋固，毋我。

BOOK NINE

1   The Master seldom spoke of profit or fate or Goodness.[1]

2   A villager from Ta-hsiang said, Master K'ung is no doubt a very great man and vastly learned. But he does nothing to bear out this reputation. The Master, hearing of it, said to his disciples, What shall I take up? Shall I take up chariot-driving? Or shall it be archery? I think I will take up driving![2]

3   The Master said, The hemp-thread crown is prescribed by ritual.[3] Nowadays people wear black silk, which is economical; and I follow the general practice. Obeisance below the daïs is prescribed by ritual. Nowadays people make obeisance after mounting the daïs. This is presumptuous, and though to do so is contrary to the general practice, I make a point of bowing while still down below.

4   There were four things that the Master wholly eschewed: he took nothing for granted,[4] he was never over-positive, never obstinate, never egotistic.

1   We may expand: Seldom spoke of matters from the point of view of what would pay best, but only from the point of view of what was right. He did not discuss whether Heaven determines all human actions (a question debated by the school of Mo Tzu in later days and evidently already raised in the time of Confucius). He refused to define Goodness or accord the title Good to any of his contemporaries.

2   See additional notes.

3   For wear at the ancestral sacrifice; made of threads twisted from a very thin yarn, very costly to manufacture.

4   Chêng Hsüan (Pelliot MS.) reads the 'man' determinative at the side of

（五）

　　子畏于匡，曰："文王既没，文不在兹乎？天之将丧斯文也，后死者不得与于斯文也。天之未丧斯文也，匡人其如予何？"

（六）

　　太宰问于子贡曰："夫人圣者与？何其多能也？"子贡曰："固天纵之将圣，又多能也。"子闻之，曰："太宰知我乎？吾少也贱，故多能鄙事。君子多乎哉？不多也。"

　　牢曰："子云：'吾不试，故艺。'"

5   When the Master was trapped in K'uang,[1] he said, When King Wên perished, did that mean that culture (*wên*) ceased to exist?[2] If Heaven had really intended that such culture as his should disappear, a latter-day mortal would never have been able to link himself to it as I have done. And if Heaven does not intend to destroy such culture, what have I to fear from the people of K'uang?

6   The Grand Minister (of Wu?)[3] asked Tzu-kung saying, Is your Master a Divine Sage? If so, how comes it that he has many practical accomplishments?[4] Tzu-kung said, Heaven certainly intended[5] him to become a Sage; it is also true that he has many accomplishments. When the Master heard of it he said, The Grand Minister is quite right about me. When I was young I was in humble circumstances; that is why I have many practical accomplishments in regard to simple, everyday matters. Does it befit a gentleman to have many accomplishments? No, he is in no need of them at all.

Lao says that the Master said, It is because I have not been given a chance[6] that I have become so handy.

---

i and interprets 'he never took anything for granted when he was not sure'. This is certainly right.

1   A border town held at various times by Chêng, Wei, Sung and Lu. For the legend as to why he was maltreated here, see additional notes.

2   Literally, 'was not in this'. cf. the common Chinese phrase 'Suppose there were a man in this', i.e. 'suppose the case of a man who . . . ', 'being in this' meaning 'existing'. cf. *Mencius*, VI, B, 2. 'Take the case of a man not strong enough to lift . . . '

3   Probably P'i (adult name, Tzu-yü), who is mentioned in connection with Tzu-kung in 488 BC.

4   Gentlemen do not stoop to practical accomplishments; much less the Sage.

5   But the wickedness of the world prevented it.

6   In public life. Lao is usually identified with the Ch'in Chang mentioned in *Tso Chuan*, Duke Chao, 20th year, and the Tzu-lao of *Chuang Tzu* XXV, 6.

（七）

子曰：“吾有知乎哉? 无知也。有鄙夫问于我，空空如也，我叩其两端而竭焉。”

（八）

子曰：“凤鸟不至，河不出图，吾已矣夫!”

（九）

子见齐衰者、冕衣裳者与瞽者，见之，虽少必作;过之，必趋。

（十）

颜渊喟然叹曰：“仰之弥高，钻之弥坚，瞻之在前，忽焉在后。夫子循循然善诱人，博我以文，约我以礼，欲罢不能。既竭吾才，如有所立卓尔，虽欲从之，末由也已。”

（十一）

子疾病，子路使门人为臣。病间，曰：“久矣哉!由之行诈也。无臣而为有臣，吾谁欺，欺天乎?且予与其死于臣之手也，无宁死于二三子之手乎?且予纵不得大葬，予死于道路乎?”

7 The Master said, Do I regard myself as a possessor of wisdom? Far from it. But if even a simple peasant comes in all sincerity and asks me a question, I am ready to thrash the matter out, with all its pros and cons, to the very end.

8 The Master said, The phoenix does not come; the river gives forth no chart.[1] It is all over with me![2]

9 Whenever he was visited by anyone dressed in the robes of mourning or wearing ceremonial headdress, with gown and skirt, or a blind man, even if such a one were younger than himself, the Master on seeing him invariably rose to his feet, and if compelled to walk past him always quickened his step.[3]

10 Yen Hui said with a deep sigh, The more I strain my gaze up towards it,[4] the higher it soars. The deeper I bore down into it, the harder it becomes. I see it in front; but suddenly it is behind. Step by step the Master skilfully lures one on. He has broadened me with culture, restrained me with ritual. Even if I wanted to stop, I could not. Just when I feel that I have exhausted every resource, something seems to rise up, standing out sharp and clear.[5] Yet though I long to pursue it, I can find no way of getting to it at all.

11 When the Master was very ill, Tzu-lu caused some of the disciples to get themselves up as official retainers.[6] Coming to himself for a short while, the Master said, How like Yu, to go in for this sort of imposture! In pretending to have retainers when I have none, whom do I deceive? Do I deceive Heaven? Not only would I far rather die in the arms of you disciples than in the arms of retainers, but also as regards my funeral – even if I am not accorded a State Burial, it is not as though I were dying by the roadside.[7]

1 The arrival of this magical bird and the sudden revelation of a magical chart were portents that heralded the rise of a Saviour Sage.

2 Heaven does not intend to let me play a Sage's part.

3 A sign of respect.

4 Goodness.

5 Literally, 'overtoppingly', like a mountain-top or the top of a tree.

6 Such as he would have been entitled to, had he held office.

7 i.e. don't think I am worrying about whether I shall be buried with

（十二）

子贡曰：　"有美玉于斯，韫椟而藏诸? 求善贾而沽诸?" 子曰：　"沽之哉，沽之哉! 我待贾者也。"

（十三）

子欲居九夷。或曰：　"陋，如之何?" 子曰：　"君子居之，何陋之有?"

（十四）

子曰：　"吾自卫反鲁，然后乐正，《雅》、《颂》各得其所。"

（十五）

子曰：　"出则事公卿，人则事父兄，丧事不敢不勉，不为酒困，何有于我哉?"

（十六）

子在川上，曰：　"逝者如斯夫! 不舍昼夜。"

（十七）

子曰："吾未见好德如好色者也。"

12 Tzu-kung said, Suppose one had a lovely jewel, should one wrap
it up, put it in a box and keep it, or try to get the best price one
can for it? The Master said, Sell it! Most certainly sell it! I myself
am one who is waiting for an offer.[1]

13 The Master wanted to settle among the Nine Wild Tribes of the
East.[2] Someone said, I am afraid you would find it hard to put up
with their lack of refinement. The Master said, Were a true
gentleman to settle among them there would soon be no
trouble[3] about lack of refinement.

14 The Master said, It was only after my return from Wei to Lu that
music was revised, Court pieces and Ancestral Recitations being
at last properly discriminated.[4]

15 The Master said, I can claim that at Court I have duly served the
Duke and his officers; at home, my father and elder brother. As
regards matters of mourning, I am conscious of no neglect, nor
have I ever been overcome with wine. Concerning these things
at any rate my mind is quite at rest.[5]

16 Once when the Master was standing by a stream, he said, Could
one but go on and on[6] like this, never ceasing day or night!

17 The Master said, I have never yet seen anyone whose desire to
build up his moral power was as strong as sexual desire.

---

public honours. I know I can trust you to give me a decent burial; and
that is all I ask for.

1   The question at issue is, of course, whether a man of talent should try
to obtain office. Confucius declares that he himself is only too anxious
to 'sell his jewel' (i.e. accept office), should any opportunity present
itself.

2   For Confucius's ideas on the 'noble savage', see V, 6 and note.

3   For *ho yu*, an idiom that cannot be translated literally, cf. VI, 6, VII, 2,
IX, 15.

4   The words of the Court pieces (*ya*) are contained in the second and
third parts, the Recitations (*sung*) in the last of the four great divisions
of the *Book of Songs*.

5   Another instance of the idiomatic *ho yu*.

6   In one's moral striving, cf. *Mencius*, IV, B, 18

(十八)

子曰：　"譬如为山，未成一篑，止，吾止也。譬如平地，虽覆一篑，进，吾往也。"

(十九)

子曰：　"语之而不惰者，其回也与!"

(二十)

子谓颜渊，曰：　"惜乎! 吾见其进也，未见其止也。"

(二十一)

子曰：　"苗而不秀者有矣夫，秀而不实者有矣夫!"

(二十二)

子曰：　"后生可畏，焉知来者之不如今也? 四十、五十而无闻焉，斯亦不足畏也已。"

(二十三)

子曰：　"法语之言，能无从乎? 改之为贵。巽与之言，能无说乎? 绎之为贵。说而不绎，从而不改，吾未如之何也已矣。"

18 The Master said, The case[1] is like that of someone raising a mound. If he stops working, the fact that it perhaps needed only one more basketful makes no difference; I stay where I am. Whereas even if he has not got beyond levelling the ground, but is still at work, the fact that he has only tilted one basketful of earth makes no difference. I go to help him.

19 The Master said, It was Hui whom I could count on always to listen attentively to anything I said.

20 The Master said of Yen Hui, Alas, I saw him go forward, but had no chance to see whither this progress would have led him in the end.[2]

21 The Master said, There are shoots whose lot it is to spring up but never to flower; others whose lot it is to flower, but never bear fruit.[3]

22 The Master said, Respect the young. How do you know that they will not one day be all that you are now? But if a man has reached forty or fifty and nothing has been heard of him, then I grant there is no need to respect him.

23 The Master said, The words of the *Fa Yü*[4] (Model Sayings) cannot fail to stir us; but what matters is that they should change our ways. The words of the *Hsüan Chü*[5] cannot fail to commend themselves to us; but what matters is that we should carry them out. For those who approve but do not carry out, who are stirred, but do not change, I can do nothing at all.

---

1 i.e. my attitude towards disciples in different stages of progress. A parallel passage in *Hsün Tzu* P'ien 28, makes the sense and construction of this passage quite clear.

2 This seems better than the traditional, 'I saw him make progress and never saw him stand still.'

3 This surely refers to Yen Hui's early death.

4 Name of a collection of moral sayings? I suspect that it is the same as the *Fa Yen* twice quoted in *Chuang Tzu* (IV, 2).

5 Name of another collection of moral sayings, on the 'choice' and 'promotion' of the virtuous?

(二十四)

子曰：　"主忠信，无友不如己者，过则勿惮改。"

(二十五)

子曰：　"三军可夺帅也，匹夫不可夺志也。"

(二十六)

子曰：　"衣敝缊袍，与衣狐貉者立，而不耻者，其由也与! '不忮不求，何用不臧?'" 子路终身诵之。子曰：　"是道也，何足以臧?"

(二十七)

子曰：　"岁寒，然后知松柏之后凋也。"

(二十八)

子曰：　"知者不惑，仁者不忧，勇者不惧。"

24 The Master said, First and foremost, be faithful to your superiors, keep all promises, refuse the friendship of all who are not like you; and if you have made a mistake, do not be afraid of admitting the fact and amending your ways.[1]

25 The Master said, You may rob the Three Armies of their commander-in-chief, but you cannot deprive the humblest peasant of his opinion.

26 The Master said, 'Wearing a shabby hemp-quilted gown, yet capable of standing unabashed with those who wore fox and badger.' That would apply quite well to Yu, would it not?

> Who harmed none, was foe to none,
> Did nothing that was not right.[2]

Afterwards Tzu-lu (Yu) kept on continually chanting those lines to himself. The Master said, Come now, the wisdom contained in them is not worth treasuring[3] to that extent!

27 The Master said,[4] Only when the year grows cold do we see that the pine and cypress are the last[5] to fade.

28 The Master said, He that is really Good can never be unhappy. He that is really wise can never be perplexed. He that is really brave is never afraid.[6]

1 cf. I, 8.

2 Confucius quotes these two lines from *Songs*, No. 67.

3 Pun on two senses of *tsang* (1) excellent; (2) treasure, to treasure up, to store.

4 He is, however, only repeating a proverb.

5 *hou* (last) should probably be *pu* or *wu* (not). A similar saying in *Lü Shih Ch'un Ch'iu* (74, 2) refers to the Master's ordeals in Ch'ên and Ts'ai. cf. *Chuang Tzu* XXVIII, 8.

6 Goodness, wisdom and courage are the Three Ways of the true gentleman. cf. XIV, 30. Confucius always ranks courage below wisdom and wisdom below Goodness. In the original the first two clauses have become transposed. This is, however, a mere slip, as is shown by comparison with the parallel passage, XIV, 30. The *Chung Yung* (*Doctrine of the Mean*), XX, in reproducing the terms in the order wisdom, goodness, courage, merely betrays the influence of this corrupted passage.

(二十九)

子曰：　"可与共学，未可与适道；可与适道，未可与立；可与立，未可与权。"

(三十)

"唐棣之华，偏其反而。岂不尔思，室是远而。"子曰："未之思也。夫何远之有?"

29 The Master said, There are some whom one can join in study but whom one cannot join in progress along the Way; others whom one can join in progress along the Way, but beside whom one cannot take one's stand;[1] and others again beside whom one can take one's stand, but whom one cannot join in counsel.

30   The flowery branch of the wild cherry
                     How swiftly it flies back![2]
                     It is not that I do not love you;
                     But your house is far away.

The Master said, He did not really love her. Had he done so, he would not have worried about the distance.[3]

---

1   i.e. with whom one cannot collaborate in office. cf. X, 3 and XVI, 13.
2   When one pulls it to pluck the blossom. cf. *Songs*, 268, 1. Image of things that are torn apart after a momentary union. Evidently a verse from some song not included in our *Book of Songs*.
3   Men fail to attain to Goodness because they do not care for it sufficiently, not because Goodness 'is far away'. I think the old interpretation, which treats 29 and 30 as one paragraph, is definitely wrong.

乡党第十

（一）

　　孔子于乡党，恂恂如也，似不能言者。其在宗庙朝廷，便便言，唯谨尔。

（二）

　　朝，与下大夫言，侃侃如也。与上大夫言，訚訚如也。君在，踧踖如也，与与如也。

（三）

　　君召使摈，色勃如也，足躩如也。揖所与立，左右手，衣前后，襜如也。趋进，翼如也。
　　宾退，必复命，曰：“宾不顾矣。”

（四）

　　入公门，鞠躬如也，如不容。立不中门，行不履阈。过位，色勃如也，足躩如也，其言似不足者。摄齐升堂，鞠躬如也，屏气似不息者。出，降一等，逞

BOOK TEN

1　At home in his native village his manner is simple and unassuming, as though he did not trust himself to speak. But in the ancestral temple and at Court he speaks readily, though always choosing his words with care.

2　At Court when conversing with the Under Ministers his attitude is friendly and affable; when conversing with the Upper Ministers, it is restrained and formal. When the ruler is present it is wary, but not cramped.

3　When the ruler summons him to receive a guest, a look of confusion comes over his face and his legs seem to give beneath his weight. When saluting his colleagues he passes his right hand to the left, letting his robe hang down in front and behind; and as he advances with quickened step, his attitude is one of majestic dignity.

　　When the guest has gone, he reports the close of the visit, saying, 'The guest is no longer looking back.'

4　On entering the Palace Gate he seems to shrink into himself, as though there were not room. If he halts, it must never be in the middle of the gate, nor in going through does he ever tread on the threshold. As he passes the Stance[1] a look of confusion comes over his face, his legs seem to give way under him and words seem to fail him. While, holding up the hem of his skirt, he ascends the Audience Hall, he seems to double up and keeps in his breath, so that you would think he was not breathing at all.

1　The place where the ruler takes up his stand when seeing off important guests?

颜色，怡怡如也。没阶，趋进，翼如也。复其位，踧踖如也。

（五）

执圭，鞠躬如也，如不胜。上如揖，下如授。勃如战色，足蹜蹜如有循。享礼，有容色。私觌，愉愉如也。

（六）

君子不以绀緅饰，红紫不以为亵服。当暑，袗絺绤，必表而出之。缁衣羔裘，素衣麑裘，黄衣狐裘。亵裘长，短右袂。必有寝衣，长一身有半。狐貉之厚以居。去丧无所不佩。非帷裳，必杀之。羔裘玄冠不以吊。吉月，必朝服而朝。

On coming out, after descending the first step his expression relaxes into one of satisfaction and relief. At the bottom of the steps he quickens his pace, advancing with an air of majestic dignity. On regaining his place he resumes his attitude of wariness and hesitation.

5 When carrying the tablet of jade,[1] he seems to double up, as though borne down by its weight. He holds it at the highest as though he were making a bow,[2] at the lowest, as though he were proffering a gift. His expression, too, changes to one of dread and his feet seem to recoil, as though he were avoiding something. When presenting ritual-presents, his expression is placid. At the private audience his attitude is gay and animated.

6 A gentleman does not wear facings of purple or mauve, nor in undress does he use pink or roan.[3] In hot weather he wears an unlined gown of fine thread loosely woven, but puts on an outside garment before going out-of-doors.[4] With a black robe he wears black lambskin; with a robe of undyed silk, fawn. With a yellow robe, fox fur.[5] On his undress robe the fur cuffs are long; but the right is shorter than the left.[6] His bedclothes must be half as long again as a man's height.[7] The thicker kinds of fox and badger are for home wear. Except when in mourning, he wears all his girdle-ornaments.[8] Apart from his Court apron, all his

1 Symbol of the ruler's feudal investiture; the *kuei*.
2 On a level with his forehead.
3 Usually translated 'purple'. But the term is applied to the coats of horses and cannot mean anything that we should call purple. These colours were reserved for times of fasting and mourning.
4 To do otherwise would be like going out into the town in one's shirt-sleeves.
5 cf. our black tie with black waistcoat.
6 To give him freedom of movement (pseudo K'ung An-kuo).
7 He does not, of course, undress, but simply draws the bedclothes over him. According to Chu Hsi this refers only to one preparing for sacrifice.
8 Which are lucky talismans; or (in a more sophisticated vein of explanations) symbolic ornaments indicating his rank. Those of an ordinary gentleman were of jade.

(七)

　　斋，必有明衣，布。斋必变食，居必迁坐。食不厌精，脍不厌细。食饐而餲，鱼馁而肉败，不食。色恶，不食。臭恶，不食。失饪，不食。不时，不食。割不正，不食。不得其酱，不食。肉虽多，不使胜食气。唯酒无量，不及乱。沽酒市脯，不食。不撤姜食。不多食。

(八)

　　祭于公，不宿肉。祭肉不出三日，出三日，不食之矣。食不语，寝不言。虽疏食菜羹瓜，祭，必斋如也。

(九)

　　席不正，不坐。

(十)

　　乡人饮酒，杖者出，斯出矣。乡人傩，朝服而立

skirts are wider at the bottom than at the waist. Lambskin dyed black and a hat of dark-dyed silk must not be worn when making visits of condolence.[1] At the Announcement of the New Moon he must go to Court in full Court dress.

7, 8.   When preparing himself for sacrifice he must wear the Bright Robe,[2] and it must be of linen. He must change his food and also the place where he commonly sits. But there is no objection to his rice being of the finest quality, nor to his meat being finely minced. Rice affected by the weather or turned he must not eat, nor fish that is not sound, nor meat that is high. He must not eat anything discoloured or that smells bad. He must not eat what is overcooked nor what is undercooked, nor anything that is out of season. He must not eat what has been crookedly cut, nor any dish that lacks its proper seasoning. The meat that he eats must at the very most not be enough to make his breath smell of meat rather than of rice. As regards wine, no limit is laid down; but he must not be disorderly. He may not drink wine bought at a shop or eat dried meat from the market. He need not refrain from such articles of food as have ginger sprinkled over them; but he must not eat much of such dishes.[3]

After a sacrifice in the ducal palace, the flesh must not be kept overnight. No sacrificial flesh may be kept beyond the third day. If it is kept beyond the third day, it may no longer be eaten. While it is being eaten, there must be no conversation, nor any word spoken while lying down after the repast. Any article of food, whether coarse rice, vegetables, broth or melon, that has been used as an offering must be handled with due solemnity.

9   He must not sit on a mat that is not straight.[4]

10   When the men of his village are drinking wine he leaves the feast directly the village-elders have left. When the men of his village

---

1   i.e., 'plain' articles must be worn, approximating to those worn by the mourner. For these rules of dress, cf. *Li Chi*, XIII, fol. 3.
2   *Ming I*, the 'spirit robe' used during the period of purification. cf. *Ming Ch'i*, 'spirit gear', the objects buried along with the dead in a tomb.
3   All the above refers to periods of preparation for sacrifice.
4   While eating sacrificial flesh?

阼阶。

(十一)

问人于他邦，再拜而送之。康子馈药，拜而受之。曰："丘未达，不敢尝。"

(十二)

厩焚，子退朝，曰："伤人乎?"不问马。

(十三)

君赐食，必正席先尝之。君赐腥，必熟而荐之。君赐生，必畜之。侍食于君，君祭先饭。疾，君视之，东首，加朝服拖绅。君命召，不俟驾行矣。

(十四)

入太庙，每事问。

(十五)

朋友死，无所归，曰："于我殡。"朋友之馈，虽车马，非祭肉不拜。

hold their Expulsion Rite,[1] he puts on his Court dress and stands on the eastern steps.[2]

11 When sending a messenger to enquire after someone in another country, he prostrates himself twice while speeding the messenger on his way. When K'ang-tzu[3] sent him some medicine he prostrated himself and accepted it; but said, As I am not acquainted with its properties, I cannot venture to taste it.[4]

12 When the stables were burnt down, on returning from Court, he said, Was anyone hurt? He did not ask about the horses.

13 When his prince sends him a present of food, he[5] must straighten his mat and be the first to taste what has been sent. When what his prince sends is a present of uncooked meat, he must cook it and make a sacrificial offering. When his prince sends a live animal, he must rear it.[6] When he is waiting upon his prince at meal-times, while his prince is making the sacrificial offering, he (the gentleman) tastes the dishes. If he is ill and his prince comes to see him, he has himself laid with his head to the East with his Court robes thrown over him and his sash drawn across the bed. When the prince commands his presence he goes straight to the palace without waiting for his carriage to be yoked.[7]

14 On entering the Ancestral Temple, he asks about every detail.[8]

15 If a friend dies and there are no relatives to fall back on, he says, 'The funeral is my affair.' On receiving a present from a friend, even a carriage and horses, he does not prostrate himself. He does so only in the case of sacrificial meat being sent.

---

1 The driving away of evil spirits at the close of the year; see additional notes.

2 The place occupied by one who is presiding over a ceremony.

3 Head of the all-powerful Chi family. This sentence and the next paragraph obviously refer to Confucius himself.

4 A *chün-tzu* takes no medicine except that administered to him by a doctor whose father and grandfather have served the family. Compare the attachment of the English *chün-tzu* to the 'old family doctor'.

5 The gentleman?

6 Not use it for food.

7 cf. *Mencius*, V, B, 7.

8 cf. III, 15.

(十六)

寝不尸，居不容。见齐衰者，虽狎必变。见冕者
与瞽者，虽亵必以貌。凶服者式之。式负版者。有盛
馔，必变色而作。迅雷风烈必变。

(十七)

升车，必正立执绥。车中不内顾，不疾言，不亲
指。

(十八)

色斯举矣，翔而后集。曰："山梁雌雉，时哉，
时哉! 子路共之，三嗅而作。"

16 In bed he avoids lying in the posture of a corpse.[1] When at home he does not use ritual attitudes. When appearing before[2] anyone in mourning, however well he knows him, he must put on an altered expression, and when appearing before anyone in sacrificial garb, or a blind man, even informally, he must be sure to adopt the appropriate attitude. On meeting anyone in deep mourning he must bow across the bar of his chariot; he also bows to people carrying planks.[3] When confronted with a particularly choice dainty at a banquet, his countenance should change and he should rise to his feet. Upon hearing a sudden clap of thunder or a violent gust of wind, he must change countenance.

17 When mounting a carriage, he must stand facing it squarely and holding the mounting-cord. When riding he confines his gaze,[4] does not speak rapidly or point with his hands.[5]

18 (The gentleman) rises and goes at the first sign,[6] and does not 'settle till he has hovered'.[7] (A song) says:

> The hen-pheasant of the hill-bridge,
> Knows how to bide its time, to bide its time!
> When Tzu-lu made it an offering,
> It sniffed three times before it rose.[8]

1 i.e. with his face to the North, where lies the land of the Dead.
2 Or 'when he sees'. For different ways of writing the expression for 'mourning garb', see *Tz'u T'ung*, 434.
3 Traditionally explained as meaning 'census tablets'.
4 Does not look about promiscuously.
5 Pointing is considered maleficent, unlucky, rude, as the case may be, in many parts of the world.
6 Of evil intentions on the part of the ruler; cf. *Lü Shih Ch'un Ch'iu*, P'ien 101, fol. 1. 'The *chün-tzu* is like a bird; if he is startled he rises.'
7 Is circumspect in choosing a new State in which to settle.
8 This quatrain (if such it is intended to be) resembles in content the songs by means of which the people commented on current political events. It is natural to interpret it as referring to the circumspect conduct of Confucius when the Chi Family (through the agency of Tzu-lu) invited him to return to Lu. One makes an offering to birds or animals whose behaviour suggests that they are sent by Heaven as omens or portents. For an anecdote of Tzu-lu and a pheasant, see *Lü Shih Ch'un Ch'iu*, 44, 1.

先进第十一

（一）

子曰：“先进于礼乐，野人也；后进于礼乐，君子也。如用之，则吾从先进。”

（二）

子曰：“从我于陈、蔡者，皆不及门也。德行：颜渊，闵子骞，冉伯牛，仲弓。言语：宰我，子贡。政事：冉有，季路。文学：子游，子夏。”

（三）

子曰：“回也，非助我者也，于吾言无所不说。”

BOOK ELEVEN

1   The Master said, 'Only common people wait till they are
    advanced in ritual and music [before taking office]. A gentleman
    can afford to get up his ritual and music later on.' Even if I
    accepted this saying, I should still be on the side of those who get
    on with their studies first.[1]

2a The Master said, My adherents in Ch'ên and Ts'ai were none of
    them in public service.[2]

2b Those who worked by moral power were Yen Hui, Min Tzu-
    ch'ien, Jan Kêng and Jan Yung. Those who spoke well were Tsai
    Yü and Tzu-kung. Those who surpassed in handling public
    business were Jan Ch'iu and Tzu-lu; in culture and learning,
    Tzu-yu and Tzu-hsia.[3]

3   The Master said, Hui was not any help to me; he accepted
    everything I said.

1   This is the interpretation of Liu Pao-nan, founded on Chêng Hsüan.
    For the contrast between *chün-tzu* and *yeh-jen* cf. *Mencius*, III, A, 3: 'If
    there were no *chün-tzu*, there would be no one to keep the common
    people (*yeh-jen*) in order; if there were no common people, there
    would be no one to produce food for the *chün-tzu*.'
2   cf. *Mencius*, VII, B, 18, where Confucius's difficulties in Ch'ên and Ts'ai
    are attributed to his being out of touch with the ruling classes in those
    States. The current interpretation 'Not one of them now comes near
    my door', taken as a complaint of their infidelity, is comparatively
    recent.
3   This classification of the disciples is not put into the mouth of
    Confucius, as is clear from the form in which the names are given.

（四）

子曰：“孝哉闵子骞！人不间于其父母昆弟之言。”

（五）

南容三复白圭，孔子以其兄之子妻之。

（六）

季康子问：“弟子孰为好学？”孔子对曰：“有颜回者好学，不幸短命死矣，今也则亡。”

（七）

颜渊死，颜路请子之车，以为之椁。子曰：“才不才，亦各言其子也。鲤也死，有棺而无椁。吾不徒行以为之椁。以吾从大夫之后，不可徒行也。”

（八）

颜渊死，子曰：“噫！天丧予，天丧予。”

（九）

颜渊死，子哭之恸。从者曰：“子恸矣。”曰：“有恸乎？非夫人之为恸而谁为？”

4 The Master said, Min Tzu-ch'ien is indeed a very good son. No one can take exception to what his parents or brothers have said of him.[1]

5 Nan Jung in reciting the *I* Song repeated the verse about the sceptre of white jade three times. (In consequence of which) Master K'ung gave him his elder brother's daughter to marry.[2]

6 K'ang-tzu of the Chi Family asked which of the disciples had a love of learning. Master K'ung replied, There was Yen Hui. He was fond of learning, but unfortunately his allotted span was a short one, and he died. Now there is none.

7 When Yen Hui died, his father Yen Lu begged for the Master's carriage, that he might use it to make the enclosure[3] for the coffin. The Master said, Gifted or not gifted,[4] you have spoken of your son and I will now speak of mine. When Li[5] died he had a coffin, but no enclosure. I did not go on foot in order that he might have an enclosure; for I rank next to the Great Officers[6] and am not permitted to go on foot.

8 When Yen Hui died, the Master said, Alas, Heaven has bereft me, Heaven has bereft me![7]

9 When Yen Hui died the Master wailed without restraint. His followers said, Master, you are wailing without restraint! He said, Am I doing so? Well, if any man's death could justify abandoned wailing, it would surely be this man's!

1 For the legend of his piety, see additional notes.
2 The Song in question is No. 271; see verse 5: A flaw in a white jade sceptre may be polished away; but a flaw in words cannot be repaired. 'Gave him his brother's daughter,' cf. V, 1.
3 See additional notes.
4 Confucius thus apologises for putting his son on a level with Yen Hui.
5 The name means 'carp-fish'. Later tradition makes him die later than Yen Hui.
6 It was the *shih* (knights, gentlemen, those who fought in chariots and not afoot) who ranked after the Great Officers, and it is possible that Confucius ranked as 'leader of the *shih*'.
7 Recorded because Confucius rarely spoke of Heaven?

（十）

颜渊死，门人欲厚葬之。子曰：“不可。”门人厚葬之。子曰：“回也，视予犹父也，予不得视犹子也。非我也，夫二三子也。”

（十一）

季路问事鬼神，子曰：“未能事人，焉能事鬼?”“敢问死。”曰：“未知生，焉知死?”

（十二）

闵子侍侧，訚訚如也。子路，行行如也。冉子、子贡，侃侃如也。子乐。“若由也，不得其死然。”

（十三）

鲁人为长府。闵子骞曰：“仍旧贯，如之何?何必改作!”子曰：“夫人不言，言必有中。”

（十四）

子曰：“由之瑟，奚为于丘之门?”门人不敬子路。

10 When Yen Hui died, the disciples wanted to give him a grand burial. The Master said it would be wrong to do so; nevertheless they gave him a grand burial. The Master said, Hui dealt with me as though I were his father. But I have failed to deal with him as though he were my son.[1] The fault however is not mine. It is yours, my friends!

11 Tzu-lu asked how one should serve ghosts and spirits. The Master said, Till you have learnt to serve men, how can you serve ghosts? Tzu-lu then ventured upon a question about the dead. The Master said, Till you know about the living, how are you to know about the dead?[2]

12a When Min Tzu-ch'ien stood by the Master's side in attendance upon him his attitude was one of polite restraint. That of Tzu-lu was one of impatient energy; that of Jan Ch'iu and of Tzu-kung was genial and affable. The Master was pleased.

12b [The Master said],[3] A man like Yu[4] never dies in his bed.

13 When the men of Lu were dealing with the question of the Long Treasury, Min Tzu-ch'ien said, What about restoring it on the old lines? I see no necessity for rebuilding it on a new plan.[5] The Master said, That man is no talker; but when he does say anything, he invariably hits the mark.

14 The Master said, Yu's zithern has no right to be in my house at all.[6] Whereupon the disciples ceased to respect Tzu-lu. The

1   Failed to assert my right to bury him in the way I thought suitable.
2   e.g. whether they are conscious, which was a much debated problem.
3   There seems to be a hiatus in the text.
4   Tzu-lu. For his death in 480 BC during the accession struggles in Wei, see *Tso Chuan*, Ai kung, 15th year. Confucius may well have said this on hearing of Tzu-lu's death. The words are usually regarded as a prophecy.
5   The point of the remark is very uncertain. See additional notes.
6   i.e. Tzu-lu has no right to call himself a follower of my Way. The *sê* was a 25-stringed zithern.

子曰：“由也升堂矣，未入于室也。”

（十五）

子贡问：“师与商也孰贤？”子曰：“师也过，商也不及。”曰：“然则师愈与？”子曰：“过犹不及。”

（十六）

季氏富于周公，而求也为之聚敛而附益之。子曰：“非吾徒也，小子鸣鼓而攻之可也。”

（十七）

柴也愚，参也鲁，师也僻，由也喭。

Master said, The truth about Yu is that he has got as far as the guest-hall, but has not yet entered the inner rooms.[1]

15 Tzu-kung asked which was the better, Shih or Shang.[2] The Master said, Shih goes too far and Shang does not go far enough. Tzu-kung said, If that is so, then Shih excels. The Master said, To go too far is as bad as not to go far enough.

16 The head of the Chi Family was richer than the Duke of Chou;[3] but Ch'iu,[4] when entrusted with the task of collecting his revenues for him, added to them and increased the yield. The Master said, He is no follower of mine. My little ones, you may beat the drum and set upon him. I give you leave.[5]

17 [The Master said], Ch'ai[6] is stupid, Shên[7] is dull-witted, Shih[8] is too formal; Yu, too free and easy.[9]

1 Tzu-lu had an abundance of courage, which is the elementary virtue of the gentleman. But he lacked the two other virtues: wisdom and Goodness.

2 i.e. Tzu-chang or Tzu-hsia.

3 Huang K'an (sixth century) says that this does not refer to Tan, legendary founder of Lu, but to a subsequent Duke of Chou. cf. however, Hsün Tzu, P'ien, 8, fol. 5, where the wealth of Tan is referred to.

4 i.e. Jan Ch'iu. The form in which the name is given suggests that these words were spoken by Confucius or a disciple and are not a statement of the compiler's.

5 This is, of course, meant metaphorically. The same anecdote occurs in Mencius, IV, A, 14.

6 Kao Ch'ai, associated with Tzu-lu in the Wei accession troubles.

7 Master Tsêng.

8 Tzu-chang. The meaning of the epithet p'i is very uncertain. See textual notes. Chu Hsi's 'it means that he was expert in ritual attitudes and deportment, but lacked sincerity' is not a philological gloss on p'i, but an application to this passage of what is said about Tzu-chang in XIX, 16.

9 Tradition represents Tzu-lu as a converted swashbuckler. See textual notes.

（十八）

子曰：　"回也其庶乎，屡空。赐不受命而货殖焉，亿则屡中。"

（十九）

子张问善人之道。子曰：　"不践迹，亦不入于室。"

（二十）

子曰：　"论笃是与，君子者乎? 色庄者乎?"

（二十一）

子路问：　"闻斯行诸?"子曰：　"有父兄在，如之何其闻斯行之?"冉有问：　"闻斯行诸?"子曰：　"闻斯行之。"

公西华曰：　"由也问闻斯行诸，子曰 '有父兄在'；求也问闻斯行诸，子曰 '闻斯行之'。赤也惑，敢问。"子曰：　"求也退，故进之；由也兼人，故退之。"

（二十二）

子畏于匡，颜渊后。子曰：　"吾以汝为死矣。"曰：　"子在，回何敢死?"

18 The Master said, Hui comes very near to it.[1] He is often empty.[2] Ssu (Tzu-kung) was discontented with his lot and has taken steps to enrich himself.[3] In his calculations he often hits the mark.

19 Tzu-chang asked about the Way of the good people.[4] The Master said, He who does not tread in the tracks[5] cannot expect to find his way into the Inner Room.

20 The Master said (of someone), That his conversation is sound one may grant. But whether he is indeed a true gentleman or merely one who adopts outward airs of solemnity, it is not so easy to say.

21 Tzu-lu asked, When one hears a maxim, should one at once seek occasion to put it into practice? The Master said, Your father and elder brother are alive. How can you whenever you hear a maxim at once put it into practice? Jan Ch'iu asked, When one hears a maxim, should one at once seek occasion to put it into practice? The Master said, When one hears it, one should at once put it into practice.

   Kung-hsi Hua said, When Yu asked, 'When one hears a maxim, should one at once put it into practice?' you said, You have a father and elder brother alive. But when Ch'iu asked, 'When one hears a maxim, should one at once put it into practice,' you said, 'When you hear it, put it into practice.' I am perplexed, and would venture to ask how this was. The Master said, Ch'iu is backward; so I urged him on. Yu is fanatical about Goodness; so I held him back.

22 When the Master was trapped in K'uang,[6] Yen Hui fell behind. The Master said, I thought you were dead. Hui said, While you are alive how should I dare to die?

---

1 To Goodness. The rest of the paragraph runs very awkwardly and is probably corrupt.
2 Hard up.
3 'Traded without official permission' is a possible interpretation.
4 Possibly a rival Way to that of Confucius.
5 Of the Ancients.
6 See above, IX, 5. The story is also found in *Lü Shih Ch'un Ch'iu*, 17.

(二十三)

　　季子然问："仲由、冉求可谓大臣与?" 子曰: "吾以子为异之问,曾由与求之问。所谓大臣者,以道事君,不可则止。今由与求也,可谓具臣矣。" 曰:"然则从之者与?" 子曰:"弑父与君,亦不从也。"

(二十四)

　　子路使子羔为费宰。子曰:"贼夫人之子。" 子路曰:"有民人焉,有社稷焉,何必读书,然后为学?" 子曰:"是故恶夫佞者。"

(二十五)

　　子路、曾皙、冉有、公西华侍坐。子曰:"以吾一日长乎尔,毋吾以也。居则曰,不吾知也。如或知尔,则何以哉?" 子路率尔而对曰:"千乘之国,摄乎大国之间,加之以师旅,因之以饥馑,由也为之,比及三年,可使有勇,且知方也。" 夫子哂之。"求,

23 Chi Tzu-jan¹ asked whether Tzu-lu and Jan Ch'iu could be called great ministers. The Master said, I thought you were going to ask some really interesting question; and it is after all only a question about Yu and Ch'iu! What I call a great minister is one who will only serve his prince while he can do so without infringement of the Way, and as soon as this is impossible, resigns. But in the present case, so far as concerns Yu and Ch'iu, I should merely call them stop-gap ministers. Tzu-jan said, So you think they would merely do what they were told? The Master said, If called upon to slay their father or their prince, even *they* would refuse.

24 Tzu-lu got Kao Ch'ai made Warden of Pi.² The Master said, You are doing an ill turn to another man's son. Tzu-lu said, What he will take charge of at Pi will be the peasants and the Holy Ground and Millet.³ Surely 'learning consists in other things besides reading books'.⁴ The Master said, It is remarks of that kind that make me hate glib people.⁵

25 Once when Tzu-lu, Tsêng Hsi, Jan Ch'iu and Kung-hsi Hua were seated in attendance upon the Master, he said, You consider me as a somewhat older man than yourselves. Forget for a moment that I am so. At present you are out of office and feel that your merits are not recognised. Now supposing someone were to recognise your merits, what employment would you choose? Tzu-lu promptly and confidently replied, Give me a country of a thousand war-chariots, hemmed in by powerful enemies, or even invaded by hostile armies, with drought and famine to boot; in the space of three years I could endow the people with courage and teach them in what direction⁶ right conduct lies.

1 Brother of the head of the Chi Family.
2 See VI, 7.
3 See additional notes.
4 In which the 'stupid' (see XI, 17) Ch'ai was not proficient.
5 The pertness of Tzu-lu's remark consists of the fact that he throws in the Master's teeth a favourite Confucian maxim. cf. I, 14 and Tzu-hsia's saying, I, 7.
6 For *fang* (direction), cf. VI, 28. Courage, it will be remembered, is the lowest of the three virtues. Next comes wisdom; next Goodness.

尔何如?" 对曰: "方六七十, 如五六十, 求也为之, 比及三年, 可使足民。如其礼乐, 以俟君子。" "赤, 尔何如?" 对曰: "非曰能之, 愿学焉。宗庙之事, 如会同, 端章甫, 愿为小相焉。" "点, 尔何如?" 鼓瑟希, 铿尔, 舍瑟而作, 对曰: "异乎三子者之撰。" 子曰: "何伤乎! 亦各言其志也。" 曰: "暮春者, 春服既成, 冠者五六人, 童子六七人, 浴乎沂, 风乎舞雩, 咏而归。" 夫子喟然叹曰: "吾与点也。" 三子者出, 曾皙后。曾皙曰: "夫三子者之言何如?" 子曰: "亦各言其志也已矣。" 曰: "夫子何哂由也?" 子曰: "为国以

Our Master smiled at him. What about you, Ch'iu? he said. Ch'iu replied saying, Give me a domain of sixty to seventy or say fifty to sixty (leagues), and in the space of three years I could bring it about that the common people should lack for nothing. But as to rites and music,[1] I should have to leave them to a real gentleman.

What about you, Ch'ih?

(Kung-hsi Hua) answered saying, I do not say I could do this; but I should like at any rate to be trained for it. In ceremonies at the Ancestral Temple or at a conference or general gathering[2] of the feudal princes I should like, clad in the Straight Gown and Emblematic Cap, to play the part of junior assistant.

Tien,[3] what about you?

The notes of the zithern he was softly fingering died away; he put it down, rose and replied saying, I fear my words will not be so well chosen as those of the other three.[4] The Master said, What harm is there in that? All that matters is that each should name his desire.

Tsêng Hsi said, At the end of spring, when the making of the Spring Clothes[5] has been completed, to go with five times six newly-capped youths and six times seven uncapped boys, perform the lustration in the river I, take the air[6] at the Rain Dance altars, and then go home singing. The Master heaved a deep sigh and said, I am with Tien.

When the three others went away, Tsêng Hsi remained behind and said, What about the sayings of those three people?

1   Which are the perquisites of the upper classes as opposed to the common people.

2   Scrupulously defined as 'Audiences' by the later ritualists, because in theory they were presided over by the Son of Heaven (the king of Chou).

3   i.e. Tsêng Hsi; he was the father of Master Tsêng.

4   Or 'I fear my choice will seem inferior to that of . . . '

5   A technical name for the clothes worn at the ceremony?

6   cf. *Mencius*, II, B, 2, where *fêng* means 'expose oneself to the wind'. Freak interpretations such as 'scatter', 'sing', 'sacrifice to the wind' are merely instances of wasted ingenuity.

礼，其言不让，是故哂之。"　"唯求则非邦也与?"
"安见方六七十如五六十而非邦也者?"　"唯赤则非邦
也与?"　"宗庙会同，非诸侯而何? 赤也为之小，孰能
为之大?"

The Master said, After all, it was agreed that each should tell his wish; and that is just what they did.

Tsêng said, Why did you smile at Yu?

The Master said, 'Because it is upon observance of ritual that the governance of a State depends; and his words were lacking in the virtue of cession.[1] That is why I smiled at him.'

'I suppose you were contrasting him with Ch'iu, who (by domain) certainly did not mean kingdom?'

'Where have you ever seen "a domain of sixty to seventy or fifty to sixty leagues" that was not a kingdom?'

'I suppose, then, you were contrasting him with Ch'ih, who was certainly not asking for a kingdom.'

'The business of the Ancestral Temple and such things as conferences and general gatherings can only be undertaken by feudal princes. But if Ch'ih were taking a minor part, what prince is there who is capable of playing a major one?[2]

---

1   *Jang*: giving up, ceding to others.
2   i.e. it is impossible to conceive of Kung-hsi Hua functioning on such an occasion except as the ruler of a Kingdom; so that, in effect, all three were asking for kingdoms.

颜渊第十二

(一)

颜渊问仁。子曰： "克己复礼为仁。一日克己复礼，天下归仁焉。为仁由己，而由人乎哉?" 颜渊曰： "请问其目。" 子曰： "非礼勿视，非礼勿听，非礼勿言，非礼勿动。" 颜渊曰： "回虽不敏，请事斯语矣。"

(二)

仲弓问仁。子曰： "出门如见大宾，使民如承大祭。己所不欲，勿施于人。在邦无怨，在家无怨。"

BOOK TWELVE

1   Yen Hui asked about Goodness. The Master said, 'He who can
     himself submit to ritual is Good.'¹ If (a ruler) could for one day
     'himself submit to ritual', everyone under Heaven would respond
     to his Goodness. For Goodness is something that must have its
     source in the ruler himself; it cannot be got from others.

     Yen Hui said, I beg to ask for the more detailed items of this
     (submission to ritual). The Master said, To look at nothing in
     defiance of ritual, to listen to nothing in defiance of ritual, to
     speak of nothing in defiance of ritual, never to stir hand or foot in
     defiance of ritual. Yen Hui said, I know that I am not clever; but
     this is a saying that, with your permission, I shall try to put into
     practice.²

2   Jan Jung asked about Goodness.³ The Master said, Behave when
     away from home⁴ as though you were in the presence of an
     important guest. Deal with the common people as though you
     were officiating at an important sacrifice. Do not do to others
     what you would not like yourself. Then there will be no feelings
     of opposition to you, whether it is the affairs of a State that you
     are handling or the affairs of a Family.⁵

---

1   In the *Tso Chuan* (Chao Kung, 12th year) Confucius is made to quote
     this as a saying from 'an old record'. The commentators, not
     understanding the archaic use of *k'o* (able to) turned *k'o chi* into 'self-
     conquest', an error fruitful in edification.
2   A formula of thanks for instruction; cf. *Mencius*, I, A, 7.
3   i.e. ruling by Goodness, not by force.
4   i.e. in handling public affairs.
5   A ruling clan, such as that of the Chi in Lu.

仲弓曰：“雍虽不敏，请事斯语矣。”

（三）

司马牛问仁。子曰：“仁者其言也讱。”曰：“其言也讱，斯谓之仁已乎?”子曰：“为之难，言之得无讱乎?”

（四）

司马牛问君子。子曰：“君子不忧不惧。”曰：“不忧不惧，斯谓之君子已乎?”子曰：“内省不疚，夫何忧何惧?”

（五）

司马牛忧曰：“人皆有兄弟，我独亡。”子夏曰：“商闻之矣，死生有命，富贵在天。君子敬而无失，与人恭而有礼，四海之内，皆为兄弟也。君子何患乎无兄弟也?”

（六）

子张问明。子曰：“浸润之谮，肤受之愬，不行焉，可谓明也已矣。浸润之谮，肤受之愬，不行焉，可谓

Jan Yung said, I know that I am not clever; but this is a saying that, with your permission, I shall try to put into practice.

3 Ssu-ma Niu[1] asked about Goodness. The Master said, The Good (*jen*) man is chary (*jen*) of speech. Ssu-ma Niu said, So that is what is meant by Goodness – to be chary of speech? The Master said, Seeing that the doing of it is so difficult, how can one be otherwise than chary of talking about it?[2]

4 Ssu-ma Niu asked about the meaning of the term Gentleman. The Master said, The Gentleman neither grieves nor fears. Ssu-ma Niu said, So that is what is meant by being a gentleman – neither to grieve nor to fear? The Master said, On looking within himself he finds no taint; so why should he either grieve or fear?

5 Ssu-ma Niu grieved, saying, Everyone else has brothers; I alone have none.[3] Tzu-hsia said, I have heard this saying, 'Death and life are the decree of Heaven; wealth and rank depend upon the will of Heaven. If a gentleman attends to business and does not idle away his time, if he behaves with courtesy to others and observes the rules of ritual, then all within the Four Seas[4] are his brothers.' How can any true gentleman grieve that he is without brothers?

6 Tzu-chang asked the meaning of the term 'illumined'. The Master said, He who is influenced neither by the soaking in of slander nor by the assault of denunciation may indeed be called illumined.[5] He who is influenced neither by the soaking in of

1 A native of Sung; brother of Huan T'ui, VII, 22.
2 Here again Confucius is evasive about the meaning of Goodness. He first puns on *jen*, 'chary', and *jen*, 'goodness'; and then in his second reply answers as though his first reply had meant 'Goodness is a thing one ought to be chary of talking about.' The implication is that the questioner had not yet reached a stage at which the mysteries of *jen* could be revealed to him.
3 This may merely mean that his brother Huan T'ui, being an enemy of Confucius, could no longer be regarded by Niu as a brother. When Niu died in 481 BC he left behind him at least three brothers.
4 That bound the universe.
5 cf. the section on posthumous titles in the *I Chou Shu*: 'He whom neither slander nor denunciation can influence is called clear-sighted', i.e. in his choice of subordinates.

远也已矣。"

（七）

子贡问政。子曰："足食，足兵，民信之矣。"
子贡曰："必不得已而去，于斯三者何先?"曰："去
兵。"曰："必不得已而去。于斯二者何先?"曰："去
食。自古皆有死，民无信不立。"

（八）

棘子城曰："君子质而已矣，何以文为?"子贡曰：
"惜乎!夫子之说君子也，驷不及舌。文犹质也，质犹
文也。虎豹之鞟，犹犬羊之鞟。"

（九）

哀公问于有若曰："年饥，用不足，如之何?"有
若对曰："盍彻乎?"曰："二，吾犹不足，如之何其
彻也?"对曰："百姓足，君孰与不足? 百姓不足，

slander nor by the assault of denunciation may indeed be called 'aloof'.

7   Tzu-kung asked about government. The Master said, Sufficient food, sufficient weapons, and the confidence of the common people. Tzu-kung said, Suppose you had no choice but to dispense with one of these three, which would you forgo? The Master said, Weapons. Tzu-kung said, Suppose you were forced to dispense with one of the two that were left, which would you forgo? The Master said, Food. For from of old death has been the lot of all men; but a people that no longer trusts its rulers is lost indeed.

8   Chi Tzu-ch'êng[1] said, A gentleman is a gentleman in virtue of the stuff he is made of. Culture cannot make gentlemen. Tzu-kung said, I am sorry, Sir, that you should have said that. For the saying goes that 'when a gentleman has spoken, a team of four horses cannot overtake his words'.[2]

       Culture is just as important as inborn qualities; and inborn qualities, no less important than culture. Remove the hairs from the skin of a tiger or panther, and what is left looks just like the hairless hide of a dog or sheep.[3]

9   Duke Ai enquired of Master Yu, saying, It is a year of dearth, and the State has not enough for its needs. What am I to do? Master Yu replied, saying, Have you not got your tithes? The Duke said, Even with two-tenths instead of one, I still should not have enough. What is the use of talking to me about tithes? Master Yu said, When the Hundred Families[4] enjoy plenty, the prince necessarily shares in that plenty. But when the Hundred Families

---

1   A statesman of Wei.
2   Common people can say what they like, and no harm is done. But a person in your position will at once be quoted as an authority. I read a full stop after *shuo*.
3   The man of good birth is potentially capable of 'patterning his coat' with culture, and thus distinguishing himself from the common herd. But good birth alone, though essential as a basis for culture, is not enough to make a gentleman in the Confucian sense.
4   All the people.

君孰与足?”

(十)

子张问崇德辨惑。子曰：“主忠信，徙义，崇德也。爱之欲其生，恶之欲其死，既欲其生，又欲其死，是惑也。”“诚不以富，亦只以异。”

(十一)

齐景公问政于孔子。孔子对曰：“君君，臣臣，父父，子子。”

have not enough for their needs, the prince cannot expect to have enough for his needs.

10 Tzu-chang asked what was meant by 'piling up moral force'[1] and 'deciding when in two minds'.[2] The Master said, 'by piling up moral force' is meant taking loyalty and good faith as one's guiding principles, and migrating to places where right prevails.[3] Again, to love a thing means wanting it to live, to hate a thing means wanting it to perish. But suppose I want something to live and at the same time want it to perish; that is 'being in two minds'.

> Not for her wealth, oh no!
> But merely for a change.[4]

11 Duke Ching of Ch'i[5] asked Master K'ung about government. Master K'ung replied saying, Let the prince be a prince, the minister a minister, the father a father and the son a son. The

1 No wonder Tzu-chang asked this question; for *ch'ung te* (a very common expression in old texts) sometimes (e.g. *Hsi Tz'u*, I, 7; *Tso Chuan*, Hsi Kung, 7th year) means 'to pile up *te*', sometimes (e.g. *Tso Chuan*, Wên Kung, 2nd year), 'to do honour to, exalt possessors of *te*'.

2 The two phrases in inverted commas rhyme, and no doubt Tzu-chang is asking for an explanation of a particular passage in an ancient rhymed text.

3 'If right prevails in a country, then serve it; if right does not prevail, then seek service elsewhere.'

4 Couplet from *Song* 105, 3, in which a lady says: I came all this long way to marry you, and you do not give me enough to eat. I shall go back to my country and home. Your thoughts are occupied with a new mate. If it is true that it is not because of her riches, then it is simply for the sake of a change. The last phrase (only for a change) is susceptible of other interpretations. But it is clearly thus that Confucius understands it, and he uses this story of a man who got a wife from a far country, and then promptly neglected her in favour of someone taken up 'simply for a change', as an example of 'being in two minds', 'not knowing one's own mind'.

5 Died 490 BC. The last of a long line of powerful and successful dukes. The closing years of his reign were clouded by the intrigues of the Ch'ên Family, which menaced the security of the dynasty (the prince

公曰：“善哉！信如君不君，臣不臣，父不父，子不子，虽有粟，吾岂得而食诸？”

（十二）

子曰：“片言可以折狱者，其由也与！”子路无宿诺。

（十三）

子曰：“听讼，吾犹人也，必也使无讼乎！”

（十四）

子张问政。子曰：“居之无倦，行之以忠。”

（十五）

子曰：“博学于文，约之以礼，亦可以弗畔矣夫！”

（十六）

子曰：“君子成人之美，不成人之恶。小人反是。”

（十七）

季康子问政于孔子。孔子对曰：“政者，正也。子帅以正，孰敢不正？”

Duke said, How true! For indeed when the
prince, the minister not a minister, the father not
not a son, one may have a dish of millet in fro
not know if one will live to eat it.[1]

12 The Master said, Talk about 'deciding a lawsuit with half a word'
– Yu is the man for that. Tzu-lu never slept over a promise.[2]

13 The Master said, I could try a civil suit as well as anyone. But
better still to bring it about that there were no civil suits![3]

14 Tzu-chang asked about public business. The Master said, Ponder
over it untiringly at home; carry it out loyally when the time
comes. (Literally, 'Home it untiringly, carry it out loyally.')

15 Repetition of VI, 25.

16 The Master said, The gentleman calls attention to the good
points in others; he does not call attention to their defects. The
small man does just the reverse of this.

17 Chi K'ang-tzu asked Master K'ung about the art of ruling.
Master K'ung said, Ruling (*chêng*) is straightening (*chêng*). If you
lead along a straight way, who will dare go by a crooked one?

---

was no longer a prince; ministers, i.e. the leaders of the Ch'ên faction,
were no longer content to be ministers); and by succession-squabbles
among his sons (the father no longer had the authority of a father; the
sons were not content to be sons).

1 Figure of speech denoting utter insecurity. Legend makes Duke Ching
haunted by the fear of death. cf. *Lieh Tzu*, VI, end. Advice very like
that which Confucius gives here was given to Duke Ching's ancestor
Duke Huan by Kuan Chung. See *Kuo Yü*, ch. VI, last fol., and *Han
Shih Wai Chuan*, X, 9.

2 'He never agreed to do anything that could not be done till next day;
for during the night circumstances might alter and prevent him from
carrying out his word.' Such is the interpretation of the early
commentators. Chu Hsi takes it in the sense of 'never putting off till
the morrow'. cf. *Shang Tzu's Su Chih*, 'dilatory government'.

3 cf. *Ta Hsüeh* (*Great Learning*), Commentary, Para. 4.

（十八）

季康子患盗，问于孔子。孔子对曰：“苟子之不欲，虽赏之不窃。”

（十九）

季康子问政于孔子，曰：“如杀无道以就有道，何如?”孔子对曰：“子为政，焉用杀? 子欲善，而民善矣。君子之德，风；小人之德，草。草上之风必偃。”

（二十）

子张问：“士何如? 斯可谓之达也?”子曰：“何哉，尔所谓达者?”子张对曰：“在邦必闻，在家必闻。”子曰：“是闻也，非达也。夫达也者，质直而好义，察言而观色，虑以下人，在邦必达，在家必达。夫闻也者，色取仁而行违，居之不疑，在邦必闻，在家必闻。”

（二十一）

樊迟从游于舞雩之下，曰：“敢问崇德修慝辨惑。”

18   Chi K'ang-tzu was troubled by burglars. He asked Master K'ung
     what he should do. Master K'ung replied saying, If only you were
     free from desire, they would not steal even if you paid them to.[1]

19   Chi K'ang-tzu asked Master K'ung about government, saying,
     Suppose I were to slay those who have not the Way in order to
     help on those who have the Way, what would you think of it?
     Master K'ung replied saying, You are there to rule, not to slay. If
     you desire what is good, the people will at once be good. The
     essence of the gentleman is that of wind; the essence of small
     people is that of grass. And when a wind passes over the grass, it
     cannot choose but bend.[2]

20   Tzu-chang asked what a knight must be like if he is to be called
     'influential'.[3] The Master said, That depends on what you mean
     by 'influential'. Tzu-chang replied saying, If employed by the
     State, certain to win fame, if employed by a Ruling Family,
     certain to win fame. The Master said, That describes being
     famous; it does not describe being influential. In order to be
     influential a man must be by nature straightforward and a lover of
     right. He must examine men's words and observe their expressions,
     and bear in mind the necessity of deferring to others.[4] Such a
     one, whether employed by the State or by a Ruling Family, will
     certainly be 'influential'; whereas the man who wins fame may
     merely have obtained, by his outward airs, a reputation for
     Goodness which his conduct quite belies. Anyone who makes
     his claims with sufficient self-assurance is certain to win fame in a
     State, certain to win fame in a Family.

21   Once when Fan Ch'ih was taking a walk with the Master under
     the trees at the Rain Dance altars, he said, May I venture to ask
     about 'piling up moral force', 'repairing shortcomings' and

1   This is a rhetorical way of saying that if K'ang-tzu did not accumulate
     valuables, he would not be robbed. But coupled with this meaning is
     the suggestion that the ruler's moral force operates directly on the
     people, as a magic, not merely as an example.
2   cf. *Mencius*, III, A, 2.
3   *Ta*, able to turn his *te* to account. See VI, 6.
4   See additional notes.

子曰：　"善哉问! 先事后得，非崇德与?攻其恶，无攻人之恶，非修慝与? 一朝之忿，忘其身，以及其亲，非惑与?"

(二十二)

樊迟问仁。子曰：　"爱人。"问知，子曰：　"知人。"樊迟未达。子曰：　"举直错诸枉，能使枉者直。"樊迟退，见子夏曰：　"向也，吾见于夫子而问知，子曰'举直错诸枉，能使枉者直'，何谓也?"子夏曰：　"富哉言乎! 舜有天下，选于众，举皋陶，不仁者远矣。汤有天下，选于众，举伊尹，不仁者远矣。"

(二十三)

子贡问友。子曰：　"忠告而善道之，不可则止，无自辱焉。"

(二十四)

曾子曰：　"君子以文会友，以友辅仁。"

'deciding when in two minds'?[1] The Master said, An excellent question. 'The work first; the reward afterwards'; is not that piling up moral force? 'Attack the evil that is within yourself; do not attack the evil that is in others.' Is not this 'repairing shortcomings'?

> 'Because of a morning's blind rage
> To forget one's own safety
> And even endanger one's kith and kin'[2]

is that not a case of 'divided mind'?

22 Fan Ch'ih asked about the Good (ruler). The Master said, He loves men. He asked about the wise (ruler). The Master said, He knows men. Fan Ch'ih did not quite understand.[3] The Master said, By raising the straight and putting them on top of the crooked, he can make the crooked straight.[4] Fan Ch'ih withdrew, and meeting Tzu-hsia said to him, Just now I was with the Master and asked him about the wise (ruler). He said, By raising the straight and putting them on top of the crooked he can make the crooked straight. What did he mean?

Tzu-hsia said, Oh, what a wealth of instruction is in those words! When Shun had all that is under Heaven, choosing from among the multitude he raised up Kao Yao,[5] and straightway Wickedness disappeared. When T'ang had all that is under Heaven, choosing from among the multitude he raised up I Yin;[6] and straightway Wickedness disappeared.

23 Tzu-kung asked about friends. The Master said, inform them loyally and guide them discreetly. If that fails, then desist. Do not court humiliation.

24 Master Tsêng said, The gentleman by his culture collects friends about him, and through these friends promotes Goodness.

---

1 See above, para. 10. Here all three phrases rhyme; the phrases supplied by Confucius also rhyme, and are presumably quotations from a didactic poem.

2 A rhyming triplet. Not knowing the full context either of the poem which the disciple quotes or of the one which Confucius utilises in his reply, we cannot hope to understand the exact force of this passage.

3 This applies only to the second answer.   4   See above, II, 19.

5   See *The Book of Songs*, p. 268.   6   See *The Book of Songs*, p. 278.

子路第十三

(一)

子路问政。子曰："先之劳之。"请益，曰："无倦。"

(二)

仲弓为季氏宰，问政。子曰："先有司，赦小过，举贤才。"曰："焉知贤才而举之?"曰："举尔所知。尔所不知，人其舍诸?"

(三)

子路曰："卫君待子而为政，子将奚先?"子曰："必也正名乎!"子路曰："有是哉，子之迂也!奚其正?"子曰："野哉由也!君子于其所不知，盖阙如也。名不正则言不顺，言不顺则事不成，事不成则礼乐不

BOOK THIRTEEN

1 Tzu-lu asked about government. The Master said, Lead them; encourage them! Tzu-lu asked for a further maxim. The Master said, Untiringly.

2 Jan Yung, having become steward of the Chi Family, asked about government. The Master said, Get as much as possible done first by your subordinates.[1] Pardon small offences. Promote men of superior capacity. Jan Yung said, How does one know a man of superior capacity, in order to promote him? The Master said, Promote those you know, and those whom you do not know other people will certainly not neglect.[2]

3 Tzu-lu said, If the prince of Wei were waiting for you to come and administer his country for him, what would be your first measure? The Master said, It would certainly be to correct language. Tzu-lu said, Can I have heard you aright? Surely what you say has nothing to do with the matter. Why should language be corrected? The Master said, Yu! How boorish you are! A gentleman, when things he does not understand are mentioned, should maintain an attitude of reserve. If language is incorrect, then what is said does not concord with what was meant; and if what is said does not concord with what was meant, what is to be done cannot be effected. If what is to be done cannot be effected,[3] then rites and music will not flourish. If rites and music

1 So that your time may not be taken up with petty preliminaries.
2 i.e. will certainly bring to your notice.
3 The 'chain argument' clanks rather heavily in English; but it is essential to preserve the form of the original.

兴，礼乐不兴则刑罚不中，刑罚不中则民无所措手足。故君子名之必可言也，言之必可行也。君子于其言，无所苟而已矣。"

(四)

　　樊迟请学稼。子曰："吾不如老农。"请学为圃。曰："吾不如老圃。"樊迟出。子曰："小人哉，樊须也! 上好礼，则民莫敢不敬；上好义，则民莫敢不服；上好信，则民莫敢不用情。夫如是，则四方之民襁负其子而至矣，焉用稼?"

(五)

　　子曰："诵《诗》三百，授之以政，不达。使于四方，不能专对。虽多，亦奚以为?"

do not flourish, then mutilations and lesser punishmen
astray. And if mutilations and lesser punishments go as
the people have nowhere to put hand or foot.

Therefore the gentleman uses only such language as is proper
for speech, and only speaks of what it would be proper to carry
into effect. The gentleman, in what he says, leaves nothing to
mere chance.[1]

4   Fan Ch'ih asked the Master to teach him about farming. The
Master said, You had much better consult some old farmer. He
asked to be taught about gardening. The Master said, You had
much better go to some old vegetable-gardener. When Fan
Ch'ih had gone out, the Master said, Fan is no gentleman! If
those above them love ritual, then among the common people
none will dare to be disrespectful. If those above them love right,
then among the common people none will dare to be disobedient.
If those above them love good faith, then among the common
people none will dare depart from the facts.[2] If a gentleman is like
that, the common people will flock to him from all sides with
their babies strapped to their backs. What need has he to practise
farming?[3]

5   The Master said, A man may be able to recite the three hundred
Songs; but, if when given a post in the government, he cannot
turn his merits to account, or when sent on a mission to far parts
he cannot answer particular questions,[4] however extensive his
knowledge may be, of what use is it to him?

1   The whole of this highly elaborate, literary paragraph bears the stamp
of comparatively late date. The links in chain-arguments of this kind
are always rhetorical rather than logical; and it would be a waste of time
to seek for a causal sequence. Later Confucian literature supplies many
examples of such rhetorical 'chains'. For *kou* (chance), see additional
notes.

2   Bear false witness in lawsuits.

3   See additional notes.

4   Besides delivering his message, he must be able to give an answer of his
own to particular enquiries relative to this message.

(六)

子曰："其身正，不令而行；其身不正，虽令不从。"

(七)

子曰："鲁卫之政，兄弟也。"

(八)

子谓卫公子荆："善居室。始有，曰：'苟合矣。'少有，曰：'苟完矣。'富有，曰：'苟美矣。'"

(九)

子适卫，冉有仆。子曰："庶矣哉"冉有曰："既庶矣，又何加焉？"曰："富之。"曰："既富矣，又何加焉？"曰："教之。"

(十)

子曰："苟有用我者，期月而已可也，三年有成。"

(十一)

子曰："'善人为邦百年，亦可以胜残去杀矣。'诚哉是言也！"

(十二)

子曰："如有王者，必世而后仁。"

6 The Master said, If the ruler himself is upright all will go well even though he does not give orders. But if he himself is not upright, even though he gives orders, they will not be obeyed.

7 The Master said, In their politics Lu and Wei are still brothers.[1]

8 The Master said of the Wei grandee Ching,[2] He dwelt as a man should dwell in his house. When things began to prosper with him, he said, 'Now they[3] will begin to be a little more suitable.' When he was better off still, he said, 'Now they will be fairly complete.' When he was really rich, he said, 'Now I shall be able to make them quite beautiful.'

9 When the Master was going to Wei, Jan Ch'iu drove him. The Master said, What a dense population! Jan Ch'iu said, When the people have multiplied, what next should be done for them? The Master said, Enrich them. Jan Ch'iu said, When one has enriched them, what next should be done for them? The Master said, Instruct them.

10 The Master said, If only someone were to make use of me, even for a single year, I could do a great deal; and in three years I could finish off the whole work.

11 The Master said, 'Only if the right sort of people had charge of a country for a hundred years would it become really possible to stop cruelty and do away with slaughter.' How true the saying is!

12 The Master said, If a Kingly Man were to arise, within a single generation Goodness would prevail.

1 On the rise of the Chou dynasty to power, Lu was given to the fourth and Wei to the seventh son of King Wên. The saying expresses, one may suppose, the disillusionment of Confucius on finding that things in Wei were no better than in Lu. In early times, however, it was understood as a commendation of Wei.
2 Flourished about 558 BC.
3 My household rites.

(十三)

子曰：　"苟正其身矣，于从政乎何有？不能正其身，如正人何？"

(十四)

冉子退朝，子曰：　"何晏也?"对曰：　"有政。"子曰：　"其事也。如有政，虽不吾以，吾其与闻之。"

(十五)

定公问：　"一言而可以兴邦，有诸?"孔子对曰：　"言不可以若是其几也。人之言曰：　'为君难，为臣不易。'如知为君之难也，不几乎一言而兴邦乎?"曰：　"一言而丧邦，有诸?"孔子对曰：　"言不可以若是其几也。人之言曰：　'予无乐乎为君，唯其言而莫予违也。'如其善而莫之违也，不亦善乎?如不善而莫之违也，不几乎一言而丧邦乎?"

13 The Master said, Once a man has contrived to put himself aright, he will find no difficulty at all in filling any government post. But if he cannot put himself aright, how can he hope to succeed in putting others right?[1]

14 Once when Master Jan came back from Court,[2] the Master said, Why are you so late? He replied, saying, There were affairs of State. The Master said, You must mean private business. If there had been affairs of State, although I am not used,[3] I too should have been bound to hear of them.

15 Duke Ting[4] asked if there were any one phrase that sufficed to save a country. Master K'ung replied saying, No phrase could ever be like that.[5] But here is one that comes near to it. There is a saying among men: 'It is hard to be a prince and not easy to be a minister.' A ruler who really understood that it was 'hard to be a prince' would have come fairly near to saving his country by a single phrase.

   Duke Ting said, Is there any one phrase that could ruin a country? Master K'ung said, No phrase could ever be like that. But here is one that comes near to it. There is a saying among men: 'What pleasure is there in being a prince, unless one can say whatever one chooses, and no one dares to disagree?'[6] So long as what he says is good, it is of course good also that he should not be opposed. But if what he says is bad, will it not come very near to his ruining his country by a single phrase?

---

1 The play on *chêng* 'to straighten, put right' and *chêng* 'to govern' makes this passage impossible to translate satisfactorily.
2 From the Court of the Chi Family, who had usurped the Duke's powers.
3 i.e. have no official post.
4 See above, III, 19.
5 The stop should come after *jo shih*.
6 This saying also occurs in *Han Fei Tzu*, P'ien, 36.

(十六)

叶公问政。子曰： "近者悦，远者来。"

(十七)

子夏为莒父宰，问政。子曰： "无欲速，无见小利。欲速则不达，见小利则大事不成。"

(十八)

叶公语孔子曰： "吾党有直躬者，其父攘羊，而子证之。" 孔子曰： "吾党之直者异于是，父为子隐，子为父隐，直在其中矣。"

(十九)

樊迟问仁。子曰： "居处恭，执事敬，与人患，虽之夷狄，不可弃也。"

(二十)

子贡问曰： "何如斯可谓之士矣?" 子曰： "行己有耻，使于四方，不辱君命，可谓士矣。" 曰： "敢问其次。" 曰： "宗族称孝焉，乡党称悌焉。" 曰： "敢

16 The 'Duke' of Shê[1] asked about government.[2] The Master said,
When the near approve and the distant approach.

17 When Tzu-hsia was Warden of Chü-fu,[3] he asked for advice
about government. The Master said, Do not try to hurry things.
Ignore minor considerations. If you hurry things, your personality
will not come into play.[4] If you let yourself be distracted by
minor considerations, nothing important will ever get finished.

18 The 'Duke' of Shê addressed Master K'ung saying, In my
country there was a man called Upright Kung.[5] His father
appropriated a sheep, and Kung bore witness against him. Master
K'ung said, In my country the upright men are of quite another
sort. A father will screen his son, and a son his father – which
incidentally[6] does involve a sort of uprightness.

19 Fan Ch'ih asked about Goodness. The Master said, In private life,
courteous, in public life, diligent, in relationships, loyal. This is a
maxim that no matter where you may be, even amid the
barbarians of the east or north, may never be set aside.

20 Tzu-kung asked, What must a man be like in order that he may
be called a true knight (of the Way)? The Master said, He who

> In the furtherance of his own interests
> Is held back by scruples,
> Who as an envoy to far lands
> Does not disgrace his prince's commission

may be called a true knight.
Tzu-kung said, May I venture to ask who would rank next?

---

1 See above VII, 18. cf. *Han Fei Tzu*, P'ien, 38 and *Mo Tzu*, P'ien, 46
(*Kêng Chu*).
2 i.e. about the tokens of good government.
3 A town in Lu.
4 For *ta*, see VI, 6.
5 A legendary paragon of honesty; see *Huai-nan Tzu*, ch. XIII, fol. 6,
where he is coupled with Wei-sheng Kao, *Han Fei Tzu*, P'ien, 49, and
Lü Shih Ch'un Ch'iu, P'ien, 54.
6 For the idiom see II, 18 and VII, 15.

问其次。"曰："言必信，行必果，硁硁然小人哉，抑亦可以为次矣。"曰："今之从政者何如?"子曰："噫!斗筲之人，何足算也。"

（二十一）

子曰："不得中行而与之，必也狂狷乎!狂者进取，狷者有所不为也。"

（二十二）

子曰："南人有言曰：'人而无恒，不可以作巫医。'善夫!'不恒其德，或承之羞。'"子曰："不占而已矣。"

The Master said, He whom his relatives commend for filial piety, his fellow-villagers, for deference to his elders. Tzu-kung said, May I venture to ask who would rank next? The Master said, He who always stands by his word, who undertakes nothing that he does not bring to achievement. Such a one may be in the humblest[1] possible circumstances, but all the same we must give him the next place.

Tzu-kung said, What would you say of those who are now conducting the government? The Master said, Ugh! A set of peck-measures,[2] not worth taking into account.

21 The Master said, If I cannot get men who steer a middle course to associate with, I would far rather have the impetuous and hasty.[3] For the impetuous at any rate assert themselves; and the hasty have this at least to be said for them, that there are things they leave undone.[4]

22 The Master said, The men of the south have a saying, 'Without stability[5] a man will not even make a good *shaman* or witch-doctor.'[6] Well said! Of the maxim: if you do not stabilise an act of *te*, you will get evil by it (instead of good), the Master said, They (i.e. soothsayers) do not simply read the omens.[7]

---

1   For *k'êng k'êng*, see XIV, 42.
2   'Mere thimblefuls', as we should say.
3   than the timid and conscientious.
4   cf. *Mencius*. VII. B. 37.
5   Play on *hêng* (1) a rite for stabilising, perpetuating the power of good omens and auspicious actions (see additional notes); (2) steadfast, in the moral sense.
6   For '*shaman* or witch-doctor' the *Li Chi* (33, fol. 3) has 'diviner by the yarrow stalks'.
7   To 'read the omens' is the first step in any undertaking. cf. our own word 'inaugurate'. In its moral application Confucius's remark means that it is not enough to embark on the Way; the real test is whether one can continue in it.

(二十三)

子曰：“君子和而不同，小人同而不和。”

(二十四)

子贡问曰：“乡人皆好之，何如?”子曰：“未可也。”“乡人皆恶之，何如?”子曰：“未可也。不如乡人之善者好之，其不善者恶之。”

(二十五)

子曰：“君子易事而难悦也。悦之不以道，不悦也。及其使人也，器之。小人难事而易悦也。悦之虽不以道，悦也。及其使人也，求备焉。”

(二十六)

子曰：“君子泰而不骄，小人骄而不泰。”

(二十七)

子曰：“刚、毅、木、讷，近仁。”

(二十八)

子路问曰：“何如斯可谓之士矣?”子曰：“切切偲偲，怡怡如也，可谓士矣。朋友切切偲偲，兄弟怡怡。”

23 The Master said, The true gentleman is conciliatory but not accommodating. Common people are accommodating but not conciliatory.[1]

24 Tzu-kung asked, saying, What would you feel about a man who was loved by all his fellow-villagers? The Master said, That is not enough.

     What would you feel about a man who was hated by all his fellow-villagers? The Master said, That is not enough. Best of all would be that the good people in his village loved him and the bad hated him.

25 The Master said, The true gentleman is easy to serve, yet difficult to please.[2] For if you try to please him in any manner inconsistent with the Way, he refuses to be pleased; but in using the services of others he only expects of them what they are capable of performing. Common people are difficult to serve, but easy to please. Even though you try to please them in a manner inconsistent with the Way, they will still be pleased; but in using the services of others they expect them (irrespective of their capacities) to do any work that comes along.

26 The Master said, The gentleman is dignified, but never haughty; common people are haughty, but never dignified.

27 The Master said, Imperturbable, resolute, tree-like,[3] slow to speak – such a one is near to Goodness.

28 Tzu-lu asked, What must a man be like, that he may be called a true knight of the Way? The Master said, He must be critical and exacting, but at the same time indulgent. Then he may be called a true knight. Critical and exacting with regard to the conduct of his friends; indulgent towards his brothers.

---

1 'Accommodating' (*t'ung*) means ready to sacrifice principles to agreement. cf. the common phrase *kou t'ung*, 'to agree somehow or other', i.e. at all costs.
2 cf. *Hsün Tzu*, P'ien, 27, end.
3 Or 'wooden', i.e. simple.

（二十九）

子曰：“善人教民七年，亦可以即戎矣。”

（三十）

子曰：“以不教民战，是谓弃之。”

29, 30 The Master said, Only when men of the right sort[1] have instructed a people for seven years ought there to be any talk of engaging them in warfare. The Master said, To lead into battle a people that has not first been instructed is to betray them.[2]

---

1   i.e. followers of the Way. The 'instruction' is, of course, in virtue, not in the use of arms.

2   cf. *Mencius*, VI, B, 8, and *Ku-liang Chuan*, Duke Hsi, 23rd year.

宪问第十四

（一）

宪问耻。子曰：“邦有道，谷；邦无道，谷，耻也。”

（二）

“克、伐、怨、欲不行焉，可以为仁矣?” 子曰：“可以为难矣，仁则吾不知也。”

（三）

子曰：“士而怀居，不足以为士矣。”

（四）

子曰：“邦有道，危言危行；邦无道，危行言逊。”

（五）

子曰：“有德者必有言，有言者不必有德。仁者必有勇，勇者不必有仁。”

BOOK FOURTEEN

1   Yüan Ssu asked about compunction.[1] The Master said, When a country is ruled according to the Way, (the gentleman) accepts rewards. But when a country is not ruled according to the Way, he shows compunction in regard to rewards.

2   Of the saying 'He upon whom neither love of mastery, vanity, resentment nor covetousness have any hold may be called Good,' the Master said, Such a one has done what is difficult;[2] but whether he should be called Good I do not know.

3   The Master said, The knight of the Way who thinks only of sitting quietly at home is not worthy to be called a knight.

4   The Master said, When the Way prevails in the land, be bold in speech and bold in action. When the Way does not prevail, be bold in action but conciliatory in speech.

5   The Master said, One who has accumulated moral power (te) will certainly also possess eloquence; but he who has eloquence does not necessarily possess moral power. A Good Man will certainly also possess courage; but a brave man is not necessarily Good.

---

1   With regard to accepting rewards. It will be remembered that it was Yüan Ssu (see above, VI, 3) who was rebuked for refusing a salary. The omission of his surname has led to the supposition that he was the compiler of this chapter.

2   cf. VI, 20.

(六)

　　南宫适问于孔子曰：羿善射，奡荡舟，俱不得其死然。禹、稷躬稼，而有天下。"夫子不答。南宫适出，子曰："君子哉若人，尚德哉若人!"

(七)

　　子曰："君子而不仁者有矣夫，未有小人而仁者也。"

(八)

　　子曰："爱之，能勿劳乎?忠焉，能勿诲乎?"

(九)

　　子曰："为命，卑谌草创之，世叔讨论之，行人子羽修饰之，东里子产润色之。"

6 Nan-kung Kuo[1] asked Master K'ung, saying, Yi[2] was a mighty archer and Ao shook the boat;[3] yet both of them came to a bad end.[4] Whereas Yü and Chi, who devoted themselves to agriculture, came into possession of all that is under Heaven.[5]

At the time our Master made no reply, but when Nan-kung had withdrawn he said, He is a true gentleman indeed, is that man! He has a right appraisal of 'virtue's power'(*te*),[6] has that man!

7 The Master said, It is possible to be a true gentleman and yet lack Goodness. But there has never yet existed a Good man who was not a gentleman.

8 The Master said, How can he be said truly to love,[7] who exacts no effort from the objects of his love? How can he be said to be truly loyal, who refrains from admonishing the object of his loyalty?

9 The Master said, When a ducal mandate was being prepared[8] P'i Ch'ên[9] first made a rough draft, Shih Shu[10] checked and revised it, Tzu-yü[11] the Receiver of Envoys amended and embellished it; Tzu-ch'an[12] of Tung-li gave it amplitude and colour.

1 Son of Mêng I Tzu; see II, 5.
2 A legendary hero. His name is cognate to the word for rainbow.
3 Shook his enemies out of it, at the great battle in which he destroyed the Shên-hsün clan.
4 Yi was slain by his minister Shu (or Cho) of Han. Shu's son Ao was in turn slain by Shao K'ang. For the legend, see *Tso Chuan*, Hsiang Kung, 4th year, and the *T'ien Wên*, verse 90.
5 For Great Yü drained the land and so made it suitable for agriculture. Hou Chi, from whom the Chou people were descended, was (as his name implies; *chi* = millet) the patron deity of agriculture.
6 As opposed to physical strength such as that displayed by Yi and Ao.
7 As a father loves a son or a prince his people.
8 In the State of Chêng.
9 Flourished in the middle of the sixth century BC.
10 Grandson of Duke Mou of Chêng; died in 506 BC.
11 Perhaps Yü Chieh, great-grandson of Duke Mou. He is the 'Receiver of Envoys Tzu-yü of Chêng' mentioned in *Tso Chuan*, Hsiang kung, 29th year.
12 See V, 15 and note.

（十）

　　或问子产。子曰：“惠人也。”问子西。曰：“彼哉，彼哉”问管仲。曰：“人也，夺伯氏骈邑三百，饭疏食，没齿无怨言。”

（十一）

　　子曰：“贫而无怨难，富而无骄易。”

（十二）

　　子曰：“孟公绰为赵、魏老则优，不可以为藤、薛大夫。”

10, 11 Someone asked about Tzu-ch'an. The Master said, A kindly[1] man! Asked about Tzu-hsi[2] he said, That man! That man! Asked about Kuan Chung[3] he said, This is the sort of man he was: he could seize the fief of Pien with its three hundred villages[4] from its owner, the head of the Po Family; yet Po, though he 'lived on coarse food'[5] to the end of his days, never uttered a single word of resentment.[6] The Master said, To be poor and not resent it[7] is far harder than to be rich, yet not presumptuous.[8]

12 The Master said, Mêng Kung Ch'o would have done well enough as Comptroller of the Chao or Wei families; but he was not fit to be a State minister even in T'êng or Hsüeh.[9]

1   The word is often used in a bad sense. Kindliness is often a feeble amends for neglect of duty. Thus Tzu-ch'an took people across the rivers in his own carriage; but he ought to have mended the bridges. *Mencius,* IV, B, 2.

2   A famous minister of the Ch'u State; assassinated in 479 BC. According to the accounts of him in the *Tso Chuan* he did and said much of which Confucius would certainly have approved. The exclamation with which his name is here received is, however, certainly one of disapprobation. The story that he prejudiced his prince against Confucius was probably merely invented to explain this passage.

3   See III, 22.

4   cf. *Hsün Tzu,* P'ien, 7, fol. 1.

5   A stock expression, merely meaning 'in humble circumstances'.

6   So great was Kuan Chung's prestige. This is the tenor of many stories about Kuan Chung. He struck with an arrow the man who was afterwards to become Duke Huan of Ch'i; yet the Duke forgave him and made him Prime Minister. He broke all the sumptuary laws; yet it never occurred to the people of Ch'i to regard him as 'presumptuous'.

7   As the head of the Po Family managed to do.

8   In which respect, according to Confucius's view (see III, 22), Kuan Chung signally failed.

9   Let alone in a great State like Lu. Mêng Kung Ch'o was a Lu politician who flourished about 548 BC. The Chao and Wei were noble families in Chin.

(十三)

子路问成人。曰："若臧武仲之智，公绰之不欲，卞庄子之勇，冉求之艺，文之以礼乐，亦可以为成人矣。"曰："今之成人者何必然，见利思义，见危授命，久要不忘平生之言，亦可以为成人矣。"

(十四)

子问公叔文子于公明贾曰："信乎，夫子不言不笑不取乎?"公明贾对曰："以告者过也。夫子时然后言，人不厌其言。乐然后笑，人不厌其笑。义然后取，人不厌其取。"子曰："其然，岂其然乎?"

13 Tzu-lu asked what was meant by 'the perfect man'. 7
said, If anyone had the wisdom of Tsang Wu C
uncovetousness of Mêng Kung Ch'o, the valour of Cﾠﾠﾠ ﾠﾠ
of P'ien[2] and the dexterity of Jan Ch'iu,[3] and had graced these
virtues by the cultivation of ritual and music, then indeed I think
we might call him 'a perfect man'.

He said, But perhaps today we need not ask all this of the
perfect man. One who, when he sees a chance of gain, stops to
think whether to pursue it would be right; when he sees that (his
prince) is in danger, is ready to lay down his life; when the
fulfilment of an old promise is exacted, stands by what he said
long ago – him indeed I think we might call 'a perfect man'.

14 The Master asked Kung-ming Chia[4] about Kung-shu Wên-tzu,[5]
saying, Is it a fact that your master neither 'spoke nor laughed nor
took'? Kung-ming Chia replied saying, The people who told
you this were exaggerating. My master never spoke till the time
came to do so; with the result that people never felt that they had
had too much of his talk. He never laughed unless he was
delighted; so people never felt they had had too much of his
laughter. He never took[6] unless it was right to do so, so that
people never felt he had done too much taking. The Master said,
Was that so? Can that really have been so?

---

1 Middle of the sixth century; grandson of Tsang Wên Chung, V, 17.
2 The paragon of legendary prowess. See *Hsin Hsü*, VIII.
3 It is very odd to find the disciple Jan Ch'iu ranged alongside of
worthies who belonged to a past generation and contrasted with the
men of 'to-day'. I suspect that some earlier member of the Jan family is
intended, perhaps Jan Shu, whose marksmanship at a battle between
Ch'i and Lu (516 BC) is mentioned in the *Tso Chuan*. The familiar
name of Jan Ch'iu might then easily have been substituted by a scribe.
4 Presumably a retainer of Kung-shu Wên-tzu.
5 Spoken of as 'very aged' in 504 BC, and apparently dead in 497 BC, the
year (according to the traditional chronology) of Confucius's first visit
to Wei, Wen-tzu's native place. See *Tso Chuan*, Ting Kung, 6th year
and 13th year.
6 Took rewards.

(十五)

子曰: "臧武仲以防求为后于鲁, 虽曰不要君, 吾不信也。"

(十六)

子曰: "晋文公谲而不正, 齐桓公正而不谲。"

(十七)

子路曰: "桓公杀公子纠, 召忽死之, 管仲不死。" 曰: "未仁乎?" 子曰: "桓公九合诸侯, 不以兵车, 管仲之力也。如其仁, 如其仁!"

(十八)

子贡曰: "管仲非仁者与? 桓公杀公子纠, 不能死, 又相之。" 子曰: "管仲相桓公, 霸诸侯, 一匡天下,

15 The Master said, Tsang Wu Chung occupied the fief of Fang and
then demanded from (the Duke of) Lu that (his brother) Wei
should be allowed to take the fief over from him. It is said that he
applied no pressure upon his prince; but I do not believe it.[1]

16 The Master said, Duke Wên of Chin could rise to an emergency,
but failed to carry out the plain dictates of ritual. Duke Huan of
Ch'i carried out the dictates of ritual, but failed when it came to
an emergency.[2]

17 Tzu-lu said, When Duke Huan put to death (his brother) Prince
Chiu, Shao Hu gave his life in an attempt to save the prince; but
Kuan Chung did not.[3] Must one not say that he fell short of
Goodness? The Master said, That Duke Huan was able to
convene the rulers of all the States without resorting to the use of
his war-chariots was due to Kuan Chung. But as to his[4]
Goodness, as to his Goodness!

18 Tzu-kung said, I fear Kuan Chung was not Good. When Duke
Huan put to death his brother Prince Chiu, Kuan Chung so far
from dying on Chiu's behalf became Duke Huan's Prime
Minister. The Master said, Through having Kuan Chung as his
Minister Duke Huan became leader of the feudal princes, uniting

---

1 In 550 BC Tsang Wu Chung, accused of plotting a revolt, was obliged
to go into exile. On his way he seized the fief of Fang, and then sent
word to the Duke offering to proceed into exile and relinquish Fang,
on condition that he should be allowed to hand the fief over to his
brother Tsang Wei. The request was granted. (Tso Chuan, Duke
Hsiang, 23rd year.) The later commentators fail to realise that 'Wei' is a
proper name and unsuccessfully attempt to turn it into wei 'to do'.
Translators have followed suit.

2 See additional notes.

3 Both Kuan Chung and Shao Hu were supporting Prince Chiu's claim
to the dukedom. Prince Hsiao Po (afterwards to become Duke Huan)
murdered his brother Prince Chiu and seized the ducal throne;
whereupon Kuan Chung, the great opportunist, transferred his allegiance
to the murderer.

4 i.e. Kuan Chung's.

民到于今受其赐。微管仲，吾其被发左衽矣。岂若匹夫妇之为谅也，自经于沟渎而莫之知也。"

(十九)

公叔文子之臣大夫僎，与文子同升诸公。子闻之，曰："可以为文矣。"

(二十)

子言卫灵公之无道也。康子曰："夫如是，奚而不丧?"孔子曰："仲叔圉治宾客，祝鮀治宗庙，王孙贾治军旅，夫如是，奚其丧!"

(二十一)

子曰："其言之不怍，则其为之也难。"

and reducing to good order all that is under Heaven; so that even today the people are benefiting by what he then did for them. Were it not for Kuan Chung we might now be wearing our hair loose and folding our clothes to the left![1] We must not expect from him what ordinary men and women regard as 'true constancy' – to go off and strangle oneself in some ditch or drain, and no one the wiser.

19 Kung-shu Wên-tzu, when summoned to office by the Duke (of Wei), brought with him and presented to the Duke his retainer Chuan,[2] the same Chuan who became a State officer. The Master hearing of it[3] said, With good reason was he accorded the title Wên.[4]

20 The Master referred to Duke Ling of Wei as being no follower of the true Way. K'ang-tzu[5] said, How is it then that he does not come to grief? Master K'ung said, He has Chung-shu Yü[6] to deal with foreign envoys and guests, the priest T'o[7] to regulate the ceremonies in his ancestral temple and Wang-sun Chia[8] to command his armies. Why then should he come to grief?

21 The Master said, Do not be too ready to speak of it,[9] lest the doing of it should prove to be beyond your powers.

1   As the barbarians do. Duke Huan stemmed the great invasion of the Ti tribes.
2   Or Hsien. It is necessary slightly to paraphrase this sentence in order to bring out the meaning with clarity.
3   As a historical event; not at the time when it happened.
4   cf. *I Chou Shu*, 54, fol. 1, 'He who helps commoners to rank and position is called Wên.' So various were Kung-shu Wên-tzu's merits that the business of choosing his posthumous title was unusually difficult. See *Li Chi*, IV, fol. 5.
5   The head of the Chi Family.
6   Known posthumously as K'ung Wên Tzu. See V, 14.
7   See VI, 14.
8   See III, 13.
9   Goodness. cf. XII, 3.

(二十二)

陈成子弑简公。孔子沐浴而朝，告于哀公曰："陈恒弑其君，请讨之。"公曰："告夫三子。"孔子曰："以吾从大夫之后，不敢不告也。君曰'告夫三子'者。"之三子告，不可。孔子曰："以吾从大夫之后，不敢不告也。"

(二十三)

子路问事君。子曰："勿欺也，而犯之。"

(二十四)

子曰："君子上达，小人下达。"

(二十五)

子曰："古之学者为己，今之学者为人。"

(二十六)

蘧伯玉使人于孔子。孔子与之坐而问焉，曰："夫子何为?"对曰："夫子欲寡其过而未能也。"使者出。子曰："使乎，使乎!"

22 When Ch'ên Hêng assassinatèd Duke Chien of Ch'i, Master
    K'ung washed his head and limbs,[1] went to Court and informed
    Duke Ai of Lu, saying, Ch'ên Hêng has slain his prince. I petition
    that steps should be taken to punish him. The Duke said, You had
    better inform the Three.[2] Master K'ung said, As I rank next to the
    Great Officers,[3] I could not do otherwise than lay this information
    before you. And now your Highness says 'Inform the Three'? He
    then went to the Three and informed them. They refused his
    petition. Master K'ung said, As I rank next to the Great Officers, I
    could not do otherwise than lay this petition before you.

23 Tzu-lu asked him how to serve a prince. The Master said, Never
    oppose him by subterfuges.[4]

24 The Master said, The gentleman can influence those who are
    above him; the small man can only influence those who are
    below him.

25 The Master said, In old days men studied for the sake of self-
    improvement; nowadays men study in order to impress other
    people.[5]

26 Ch'ü Po Yü[6] sent a messenger to Master K'ung. Master K'ung
    bade the man be seated and asked of him saying, What is your
    master doing? He replied, saying, My master is trying to diminish
    the number of his failings;[7] but he has not hitherto been
    successful. When the messenger had gone away, the Master said,
    What a messenger, what a messenger![8]

1   As became a suppliant. The assassination took place in 481 BC.
2   The heads of the three great families Chi, Shu and Mêng.
3   cf. XI, 7. This anecdote, in a very similar form, occurs in the *Tso
    Chuan*, Ai, 14th year.
4   But if you have to oppose him, do so openly.
5   cf. *Hsün Tzu*, P'ien, 1.
6   A famous Wei minister. See below, XV, 6.
7   Or 'is trying to lessen his offence'. Chü Po Yü may have promised to
    get Confucius a post in Wei and failed to do so. The message may mean
    that he is still trying, but has not yet succeeded arranging anything.
8   This is usually taken as an exclamation of approval. I very much doubt
    if that is so.

（二十七）

子曰：“不在其位，不谋其政。”

（二十八）

曾子曰：“君子思不出其位。”

（二十九）

子曰：“君子耻其言而过其行。”

（三十）

子曰：“君子道者三，我无能焉。仁者不忧，知者不惑，勇者不惧。”子贡曰：“夫子自道也。”

（三十一）

子贡方人。子曰：“赐也贤乎哉，夫我则不暇。”

（三十二）

子曰：“不患人之不己知，患其不能也。”

（三十三）

子曰：“不逆诈，不忆不信，抑亦先觉者，是贤乎！”

（三十四）

微生亩谓孔子曰：“丘何为是栖栖者与?无乃为佞

27, 28 When the Master said, He who holds no rank in a State does not discuss its policies,[1] Master Tsêng said, A true gentleman, even in his thoughts, never departs from what is suitable to his rank.[2]

29 The Master said, A gentleman is ashamed to let his words outrun his deeds.

30 The Master said, The Ways of the true gentleman are three. I myself have met with success in none of them. For he that is really Good is never unhappy, he that is really wise is never perplexed, he that is really brave is never afraid. Tzu-kung said, That, Master, is your own Way![3]

31 Tzu-kung was always criticising other people. The Master said, It is fortunate for Ssu that he is so perfect himself as to have time to spare for this. I myself have none.

32 The Master said, (A gentleman) does not grieve that people do not recognise his merits; he grieves at his own incapacities.

33 The Master said, Is it the man who 'does not count beforehand upon the falsity of others nor reckon upon promises not being kept', or he who is conscious beforehand of deceit, that is the true sage?[4]

34 Wei-shêng Mou said to Master K'ung, Ch'iu,[5] what is your object in going round perching now here, now there? Is it not

---

1   See above, VIII, 14.
2   Tsêng illustrates Confucius's saying by quoting an old maxim, which also figures, in practically identical form, in the first appendix (*Hsiang*) of the *Book of Changes*, section 52.
3   Is precisely how you yourself behave. Usually taken as referring to Confucius's disclaimer ('I myself have met with success in none,' etc.) and meaning, 'So you yourself say; (but we know that is only due to your modesty, and do not take your words literally).'
4   See additional notes.
5   Familiar name of Confucius, the form of address is discourteous. It is surmised that Wei-shêng Mou was a recluse.

乎?"孔子对曰: "非敢为佞也, 疾固也。"

(三十五)

子曰: "骥不称其力, 称其德也。"

(三十六)

或曰: "以德报怨, 何如?" 子曰: "何以报德? 以直报怨, 以德报德。"

(三十七)

子曰: "莫我知也夫!" 子贡曰: "何为其莫知子也?" 子曰: "不怨天, 不尤人, 下学而上达。知我者其天乎!"

(三十八)

公伯寮愬子路于季孙。子服景伯以告, 曰: "夫子固有惑志于公伯寮, 吾力犹能肆诸市朝。" 子曰: "道之将行也与, 命也; 道之将废也与, 命也。公伯寮其如命何?"

simply to show off the fact that you are a clever talker? Master K'ung said, I have no desire to be thought a clever talker; but I do not approve of obstinacy.[1]

35 The Master said, The horse Chi[2] was not famed for its strength but for its inner qualities (*te*).

36 Someone said, What about the saying 'Meet resentment with inner power (*te*)'?[3] The Master said, In that case, how is one to meet inner power? Rather, meet resentment with upright dealing and meet inner power with inner power.

37 The Master said, The truth is, no one knows me![4] Tzu-kung said, What is the reason that you are not known? The Master said, I do not 'accuse Hea ven, nor do I lay the blame on men'.[5]

But the studies[6] of men here below are felt on high, and perhaps after all I am known; not here, but in Heaven !

38 Kung-po Liao spoke against Tzu-lu to the Chi Family. Tzu-fu Ching-po[7] informed the Master saying, I fear my master's[8] mind has been greatly unsettled by this. But in the case of Kung-po Liao, I believe my influence is still great enough to have his carcase exposed in the market-place. The Master said, If it is the will of Heaven that the Way shall prevail, then the Way will prevail. But if it is the will of Heaven that the Way should perish, then it must needs perish. What can Kung-po Liao do against Heaven's will?

1 It is no use going on and on trying to convert a prince. After a time one must give it up, and try elsewhere.
2 A famous horse of ancient times. A rhymed couplet.
3 The same saying is utilised in the *Tao Tê Ching*, ch. 63. It originally meant 'Let the ruler meet discontent among his subjects with *te* and not with violence.' Confucius here uses it in a much more general sense.
4 No ruler recognises my merits and employs me.
5 'A gentleman neither accuses Heaven nor blames men.' *Mencius*, II, B, 13.
6 The self-training consisting in the study of antiquity.
7 A retainer of the Chi Family, friendly with Tzu-kung.
8 Chi K'ang-tzu's.

（三十九）

　　子曰：“贤者避世，其次避地，其次避色，其次避言。”

（四十）

　　子曰：“作者七人矣。”

（四十一）

　　子路宿于石门。晨门曰：“奚自?”子路曰：“自孔氏。”曰：“是知其不可而为之者与?”

（四十二）

　　子击磬于卫，有荷蒉而过孔子之门者，曰：“有心哉，击磬乎!”既而曰：“鄙哉，硁硁乎!莫己知也，斯己而已矣。深则厉，浅则揭。”子曰：“果哉!末之难矣。”

39 The Master said, Best of all, to withdraw from one's g
    next to withdraw to another land; next to leave be
    look; next best to leave because of a word.[1]

40 The Master said, The makers[2] were seven . . .

41 Tzu-lu was spending the night at the Stone Gates.[3] The gate-
    keeper said, Where are you from? Tzu-lu said, From Master
    K'ung's. The man said, He's the one who 'knows it's no use, but
    keeps on doing it', is that not so?

42 The Master was playing the stone-chimes, during the time when
    he was in Wei. A man carrying a basket passed the house where
    he and his disciples had established themselves. He said, How
    passionately he beats his chimes! When the tune was over, he
    said, How petty and small-minded![4] A man whose talents no
    one recognises has but one course open to him – to mind his
    own business! 'If the water is deep, use the stepping-stones; if it is
    shallow, then hold up your skirts.'[5] The Master said, That is
    indeed[6] an easy way out!

1   This continues the theme of the last paragraph. If *Tao* (the Way) does
    not prevail, it is better to flee altogether from the men of one's
    generation, rather than to go round 'perching first here, then there' as
    Confucius himself had unsuccessfully done, or to wait till the expression
    of the ruler's face betrays that he is meditating some enormity, or worst
    of all, to wait till his words actually reveal his intention.

2   i. e. inventors, 'culture-heroes', originators of fire, agriculture, metallurgy,
    boats, carriages, the potter's wheel, the loom. Their names are
    variously given. It is natural to suppose that the compilers could not
    agree as to which names Confucius had enumerated, and therefore left
    the paragraph unfinished.

3   On the frontiers of Lu and Ch'i? Both this and the next paragraph
    belong to popular legend rather than to the traditions of the school. cf.
    Book XVIII.

4   cf. XIII, 20. He sees in Confucius's passionate playing an expression of
    discontent at his failure to get office.

5   In *Song* 54. The meaning here is, 'Take the world as you find it.'

6   *Kuo* here means '*en effet*', not 'effective', 'resolute'. cf. *Mencius*,
    IV, B, 32.

(四十三)

子张曰： "《书》云： '高宗谅阴，三年不言。' 何谓也?" 子曰： "何必高宗，古之人皆然。君薨，百官总己以听于冢宰，三年。"

(四十四)

子曰： "上好礼，则民易使也。"

(四十五)

子路问君子。子曰： "修己以敬。" 曰： "如斯而已乎?" 曰： "修己以安人。" 曰： "如斯而已乎?" 曰： "修己以安百姓。修己以安百姓，尧、舜其犹病诸。"

(四十六)

原壤夷俟。子曰： "幼而不逊悌，长而无述焉，老而不死，是为贼。" 以杖叩其胫。

43 Tzu-chang said, The Books[1] say, 'When Kao Tsung was in the
    Shed of Constancy,[2] he did not speak for three years.' What does
    this mean? The Master said, Not Kao Tsung in particular. All the
    men of old did this. Whenever a prince died, the ministers (of
    the last prince) all continued in their offices, taking their orders
    from the Prime Minister;[3] and this lasted for three years.

44 The Master said, So long as the ruler loves ritual,[4] the people will
    be easy to handle.

45 Tzu-lu asked about the qualities of a true gentleman. The Master
    said, He cultivates in himself the capacity to be diligent in his
    tasks. Tzu-lu said, Can he not go further than that? The Master
    said, He cultivates in himself the capacity to ease the lot of other
    people.[5] Tzu-lu said, Can he not go further than that? The
    Master said, He cultivates in himself the capacity to ease the lot of
    the whole populace. If he can do that, could even Yao or Shun
    find cause to criticise him?[6]

46 Yüan Jang sat waiting for the Master in a sprawling position.[7]
    The Master said, Those who when young show no respect to
    their elders achieve nothing worth mentioning when they grow
    up. And merely to live on, getting older and older, is to be a
    useless pest.[8]
        And he struck him across the shins with his stick.

---

1 See *Shu Ching*, Wu Yi. cf. *Kuo Yü*, 20, fol. 2.
2 i.e. in mourning for his father. The *liang-an* was a penthouse set up for
   the habitation of a mourner against the wall of a tomb. Kao Tsung's
   traditional date is 1324–1266 BC.
3 cf. *Mencius*, III, A, 2.
4 i.e. carries on immemorial usages and customs.
5 Other gentlemen.
6 cf. VI, 28.
7 Whereas he ought to have been standing when his teacher arrived and
   only to have sat down when told to do so.
8 This paragraph is usually translated in a way which makes it appear that
   Yüan Jang was an old man, whom Confucius brutally reproaches with
   'being old and not dying'. It is, on the contrary, clear that he was a
   young man, like the boy of the next paragraph.

(四十七)

阙党童子将命。或问之曰： "益者与?" 子曰： "吾见其居于位也，见其与先生并行也。非求益者也，欲速成者也。"

47 A boy from the village of Ch'uëh used to come with messages. Someone asked about him, saying, Is he improving himself ?[1] The Master said, Judging by the way he sits in grown-up people's places and walks alongside of people older than himself, I should say he was bent upon getting on quickly rather than upon improving himself.

1   i.e. taking advantage of his visits to the house of Confucius.

卫灵公第十五

(一)

卫灵公问陈于孔子。孔子对曰： "俎豆之事，则尝闻之矣；军旅之事，未之学也。"明日遂行。在陈绝粮，从者病，莫能兴。子路愠见，曰："君子亦有穷乎？"子曰："君子固穷，小人穷斯滥矣。"

(二)

子曰："赐也，女以予为多学而识之者与？"对曰："然，非与？"曰："非也，予一以贯之。"

(三)

子曰："由，知德者鲜矣。"

BOOK FIFTEEN

1 Duke Ling of Wei asked Master K'ung about the marshalling of troops. Master K'ung replied saying, About the ordering of ritual vessels I have some knowledge; but warfare is a thing I have never studied. Next day he resumed his travels.[1] In Ch'ên supplies fell short and his followers became so weak that they could not drag themselves on to their feet. Tzu-lu came to the Master and said indignantly, Is it right that even gentlemen should be reduced to such straits? The Master said, A gentleman can withstand hardships; it is only the small man who, when submitted to them, is swept off his feet.[2]

2 The Master said, Ssu,[3] I believe you look upon me as one whose aim is simply to learn and retain in mind as many things as possible. He replied, That is what I thought. Is it not so? The Master said, No; I have one (thread) upon which I string them all.[4]

3 The Master said, Yu,[5] those who understand moral force (te) are few.

1 There is a similar story in the *Tso Chuan*, Ai Kung, 11th year.
2 As though by a flood.
3 Familiar name of Tzu-kung.
4 cf. IV, 15.
5 Familiar name of Tzu-lu.

(四)

　　子曰：　"无为而治者，其舜也与! 夫何为哉? 恭己正南面而已矣。"

(五)

　　子张问行。子曰：　"言忠信，行笃敬，虽蛮貊之邦行矣。言不忠信，行不笃敬，虽州里行乎哉? 立则见其参于前也，在舆则见其倚于衡也，夫然后行。"子张书诸绅。

(六)

　　子曰：　"直哉史鱼! 邦有道，如矢；邦无道，如矢。君子哉蘧伯玉! 邦有道，则仕；邦无道，则可卷而怀之。"

4   The Master said, Among those that 'ruled by inactivity'[1] surely
     Shun may be counted. For what action did he take? He merely
     placed himself gravely and reverently with his face due south;[2]
     that was all.

5   Tzu-chang asked about getting on with people. The Master said,
     Be loyal and true to your every word, serious and careful in all
     you do; and you will get on well enough, even though you find
     yourself among barbarians. But if you are disloyal and
     untrustworthy in your speech, frivolous and careless in your acts,
     even though you are among your own neighbours, how can you
     hope to get on well? When standing,[3] see these principles ranged
     before you; in your carriage, see them resting on the yoke. Then
     you may be sure that you will get on. Tzu-chang accordingly
     inscribed the maxim upon his sash.

6   The Master said, Straight and upright indeed was the recorder
     Yü![4] When the Way prevailed in the land he was (straight) as an
     arrow; when the Way ceased to prevail, he was (straight) as an
     arrow. A gentleman indeed is Ch'ü Po Yü.[5] When the Way
     prevailed in his land, he served the State; but when the Way
     ceased to prevail, he knew how to 'wrap it[6] up and hide it in the
     folds of his dress'.

1   *Wu-wei*, the phrase applied by the Taoists to the immobility of self-
     hypnosis.
2   The position of the ruler. Shun was a Divine Sage (*shêng*) whose *te*
     was so great that it sufficed to guide and transform the people.
3   In your place at Court.
4   Having failed to persuade Duke Ling of Wei to use the services of
     Ch'ü Po Yü, the recorder Yü gave directions that when he (the
     recorder) died his body should not receive the honours due to a
     minister, as a posthumous protest against the Duke Ling's offences. The
     story is told in *Han Shih Wai Chuan*, 7, and many other places.
5   Ch'ü Po Yü left Wei owing to the tyrannical conduct of Duke Hsien
     in 559 BC. No tense is expressed in the first clause. I say 'is' because in
     XIV, 26, Ch'ü Po Yü appears to be still alive. It is, however, not very
     probable that he was, as legend asserts, still alive when Confucius
     visited Wei in 495 BC
6   His jewel; i.e. his talents.

(七)

子曰："可与言而不与之言，失人；不可与言而与之言，失言。知者不失人，亦不失言。"

(八)

子曰："志士仁人，无求生以害仁，有杀身以成仁。"

(九)

子贡问为仁。子曰："工欲善其事，必先利其器。居是邦也，事其大夫之贤者，友其士之仁者也。"

(十)

颜渊问为邦。子曰："行夏之时，乘殷之辂，服周之冕，乐则《韶》舞。放郑声，远佞人。郑声淫，佞人殆。"

7   The Master said, Not to talk to[1] one who could be talked ⌐
    to waste a man. To talk to those who cannot be talked to, ⌐
    waste one's words. 'He who is truly wise never wastes a man ;[2]
    but on the other hand, he never wastes his words.

8   The Master said, Neither the knight who has truly the heart of a
    knight nor the man of good stock who has the qualities that
    belong to good stock[3] will ever seek life at the expense of
    Goodness; and it may be that he has to give his life in order to
    achieve Goodness.

9   Tzu-kung asked how to become Good. The Master said, A
    craftsman, if he means to do good work, must first sharpen his
    tools. In whatever State you dwell

>   Take service with such of its officers as are worthy,
>   Make friends with such of its knights as are Good.

10 Yen Hui asked about the making of a State. The Master said,
    One would go by the seasons of Hsia;[4] as State-coach for the
    ruler one would use that of Yin,[5] and as head-gear of ceremony
    wear the Chou hat.[6] For music one would take as model the
    Succession Dance,[7] and would do away altogether with the tunes
    of Chêng;[8] one would also keep clever talkers at a distance. For
    the tunes of Chêng are licentious and clever talkers are dangerous.

1   About the Way. cf. VII, 28.
2   I suspect that this is a proverbial saying.
3   The written forms of *chih* and *jen* are here half-punningly insisted upon.
4   It was believed that in the Hsia dynasty the year began in the spring.
5   Which were less ornate than those of Chou, say the commentators.
    But this is a mere guess. *Han Fei Tzu*, P'ien, 10, says that the Yin
    invented state coaches.
6   Which had some resemblance to our scholastic mortar-board.
7   See above, III, 25 and VII, 13.
8   The words to these tunes are in the seventh book of the *Songs*. But it
    was probably to the character of the music not to that of the words that
    Confucius objected. See additional notes.

（十一）

子曰：　"人无远虑，必有近忧。"

（十二）

子曰：　"已矣乎! 吾未见好德如好色者也。"

（十三）

子曰：　"臧文仲其窃位者与!知柳下惠之贤而不与立也。"

（十四）

子曰：　"躬自厚而薄责于人，则远怨矣。"

（十五）

子曰：　"不曰'如之何，如之何'者，吾末如之何也已矣。"

（十六）

子曰：　"群居终日，言不及义，好行小慧，难矣哉!"

（十七）

子曰：　"君子义以为质，礼以行之，逊以出之，信以成之。君子哉!"

（十八）

子曰：　"君子病无能焉，不病人之不己知也。"

11 The Master said, He who will not worry about what is far will soon find something worse [1] than worry close at hand.

12 The Master said, In vain have I looked for one whose desire to build up his moral power was as strong as sexual desire. [2]

13 The Master said, Surely one would not be wrong in calling Tsang Wên Chung [3] a stealer of other men's ranks? He knew that Liu-hsia Hui was the best man for the post, yet would not have him as his colleague. [4]

14 The Master said, To demand much from oneself and little from others is the way (for a ruler) to banish discontent.

15 The Master said, If a man does not continually ask himself 'What am I to do about this, what am I to do about this?' there is no possibility of my doing anything about him.

16 The Master said, Those who are capable of spending a whole day together without ever once discussing questions of right or wrong, but who content themselves [5] with performing petty acts of clemency, are indeed difficult. [6]

17 The Master said, The gentleman who takes the right as his material to work upon and ritual as the guide in putting what is right into practice, who is modest in setting out his projects and faithful in carrying them to their conclusion, he indeed is a true gentleman.

18 The Master said, A gentleman is distressed by his own lack of capacity; he is never distressed at the failure of others to recognise his merits.

---

1 *Yu* is a much stronger word than *lü*.
2 cf. IX, 17.
3 See V, 17.
4 'Degraded him', says the *Tso Chuan*, Wên Kung, 2nd year. For Liu-hsia Hui, see below, XVIII, 2.
5 'Satisfy their consciences', as we should say.
6 To lead into the Way.

（十九）

子曰：　"君子疾没世而名不称焉。"

（二十）

子曰：　"君子求诸己，小人求诸人。"

（二十一）

子曰：　"君子矜而不争，群而不党。"

（二十二）

子曰：　"君子不以言举人，不以人废言。"

（二十三）

子贡问曰：　"有一言而可以终身行之者乎?"　子曰：
"其恕乎! 己所不欲，勿施于人。"

（二十四）

子曰：　"吾之于人也，谁毁谁誉? 如有所誉者，其
有所试矣。斯民也，三代之所以直道而行也。"

（二十五）

子曰：　"吾犹及史之阙文也。有马者借人乘之，
今则亡矣夫!"

19 The Master said, A gentleman has reason to be distressed if he ends his days without making a reputation for himself.[1]

20 The Master said, The demands that a gentleman makes are upon himself; those that a small man makes are upon others.[2]

21 The Master said, A gentleman is proud, but not quarrelsome, allies himself with individuals, but not with parties.

22 The Master said, A gentleman does not

> Accept men because of what they say,
> Nor reject sayings, because the speaker is what he is.

23 Tzu-kung asked saying, Is there any single saying that one can act upon all day and every day?[3] The Master said, Perhaps the saying about consideration:[4] 'Never do to others what you would not like them to do to you.'[5]

24 The Master said, In speaking of the men of the day I have always refrained from praise and blame alike. But if there is indeed anyone whom I have praised, there is a means by which he may be tested. For the common people here round us are just such stuff as the three dynasties[6] worked upon in the days when they followed the Straight Way.

25 The Master said, I can still remember the days when a scribe left blank spaces,[7] and when someone using a horse (for the first time)[8] hired a man to drive it.[9] But that is all over now!

---

1 Which contradicts the saying before. As both sayings completely lack context, it would be a waste of time to try to reconcile the contradiction.

2 This is a proverbial saying, capable of many interpretations. To the Taoists it meant 'Seek Tao in yourself (through the practice of quietism) and not in the outside world.'

3 For *chung shên*. cf. IX, 26.

4 Ch. IV, 15.   5   cf. V, II.   6   Hsia, Yin and Chou.

7 When in doubt; instead of trusting to his imagination.

8 Some such words must have slipped out. Pao Hsien's (first century AD) commentary suggests that they were still there in his text.

9 Another instance of diffidence, parallel to 'leaving blanks'. See additional notes.

(二十六)

子曰："巧言乱德。小不忍乱大谋。"

(二十七)

子曰："众恶之，必察焉；众好之，必察焉。"

(二十八)

子曰："人能弘道，非道弘人。"

(二十九)

子曰："过而不改，是谓过矣。"

(三十)

子曰："吾尝终日不食，终夜不寝，以思，无益，不如学也。"

(三十一)

子曰："君子谋道不谋食。耕也，馁在其中矣。学也，禄在其中矣。君子忧道不忧贫也。"

(三十二)

子曰："知及之，仁不能守之，虽得之，必失之。知及之，仁能守之，不庄以莅之，则民不敬。知及之，

26 The Master said, Clever talk can confound the workings of moral force, just as small impatiences can confound great projects.

27 The Master said, When everyone dislikes a man, enquiry is necessary; when everyone likes a man, enquiry is necessary.

28 The Master said, A man can enlarge his Way; but there is no Way that can enlarge a man.[1]

29 The Master said, To have faults and to be making no effort to amend them is to have faults indeed![2]

30 The Master said, I once spent a whole day without food and a whole night without sleep, in order to meditate.[3] It was no use. It is better to learn.[4]

31 The Master said, A gentleman, in his plans, thinks of the Way; he does not think how he is going to make a living. Even farming sometimes entails[5] times of shortage; and even learning may incidentally lead to high pay. But a gentleman's anxieties concern the progress of the Way; he has no anxiety concerning poverty.

32 The Master said, He whose wisdom brings him into power, needs Goodness to secure that power. Else, though he get it, he will certainly lose it. He whose wisdom brings him into power and who has Goodness whereby to secure that power, if he has not dignity wherewith to approach the common people, they will not respect him. He whose wisdom has brought him into

---

1 Without effort on his part. Play on 'Way' and 'road'. 'A man can widen a road . . . ,' etc.

2 Whereas one should never condemn one who is amending his faults. The *Ku-liang Chuan* (Hsi, 22) adds two words, which give a very different turn to the saying.

3 See II, 15.

4 This paragraph reads at first sight as though it were the record of a personal experience. In reality it is meant in a much more general way. *Hsün Tzu* (P'ien, i, fol. 2) quotes the proverb 'I spent a whole day meditating; I should have done better to learn. I stood on tip-toe in order to get a good view; I should have done better to climb a hill.'

5 For the idiom, see II, 18; VII, 15; XIII, 18 and XIX, 6,

仁能守之，庄以莅之，动之不以礼，未善也。"

（三十三）

子曰："君子不可小知，而可大受也。小人不可大受，而可小知也。"

（三十四）

子曰："民之于仁也，甚于水火。水火，吾见蹈而死者矣，未见蹈仁而死者也。"

（三十五）

子曰："当仁不让于师。"

（三十六）

子曰："君子贞而不谅。"

（三十七）

子曰："事君，敬其事而后其食。"

power, who has Goodness whereby to secure th[...] power and dignity wherewith to approach the common people, if h[...] handle them contrary to the prescriptions of ritual, is still a bad ruler.[1]

33 The Master said, It is wrong for a gentleman to have knowledge of menial matters[2] and proper that he should be entrusted with great responsibilities. It is wrong for a small man to be entrusted with great responsibilities, but proper that he should have a knowledge of menial matters.

34 The Master said, Goodness is more to the people than water and fire. I have seen men lose their lives when 'treading upon' water and fire; but I have never seen anyone lose his life through 'treading upon' Goodness.[3]

35 The Master said, When it comes to Goodness one need not avoid competing with one's teacher.

36 The Master said, From a gentleman consistency is expected, but not blind fidelity.

37 The Master said, In serving one's prince one should be

> Intent upon the task,
> Not bent upon the pay.

1 This paragraph with its highly literary, somewhat empty elaboration, and its placing of ritual on a pinnacle far above Goodness, is certainly one of the later additions to the book. For the chain-like rhetorical development, cf. XIII, 3.

2 The usual interpretation is 'It is impossible for us to recognise a gentleman when he is merely employed in small matters'. But I do not see how such a sense can be forced out of the text as it stands. For the undesirability of a gentleman's having miscellaneous accomplishments, cf. IX, 6.

3 A symbolic 'treading upon fire' is still used in China as a rite of purification. According to the Lun-hêng (P'ien, 45) a processional wading along the river was part of the rain-making ceremony. Confucius says that Goodness (on the part of the ruler) is a greater and safer purifier than even water or fire.

（三十八）

子曰：　"有教无类。"

（三十九）

子曰：　"道不同，不相为谋。"

（四十）

子曰：　"辞，达而已矣。"

（四十一）

师冕见，及阶，子曰：　"阶也。"及席也，子曰：
"席也。"皆坐，子告之曰：　"某在斯，某在斯。"
师冕出，子张问曰：　"与师言之道与?"子曰：　"然，
固相师之道也。"

38 The Master said, There is a difference[1] in instruction but none in kind.

39. The Master said, With those who follow a different Way it is useless to take counsel.

40 The Master said, In official speeches[2] all that matters is to get one's meaning through.

41 The Music-master Mien came to see him. When he reached the steps, the Master said, Here are the steps.[3] When he reached the mat, the Master said, Here is the mat. When everyone was seated the Master informed him saying, So-and-so is here, So-and-so is there. When the Music-master Mien had gone, Tzu-chang asked saying, 'Is that the recognised way to talk to a Music-master?' The Master said, Yes, certainly it is the recognised way to help a Music-master.

1   Between us and the Sages. Any of us could turn into a Yao or Shun, if we trained ourselves as they did. cf. XVII, 2, and *Mencius*, II, A, 2.
2   *Tz' u* means pleas, messages, excuses for being unable to attend to one's duties, etc.
3   Music-masters were blind.

季氏第十六

（一）

　　季氏将伐颛臾。冉有、季路见于孔子，曰："季氏将有事于颛臾。"孔子曰："求！无乃尔是过与？夫颛臾，昔者先王以为东蒙主，且在邦域之中矣，是社稷之臣也。何以伐为？"冉有曰："夫子欲之，吾二臣者皆不欲也。"孔子曰："求！周任有言曰：'陈力就列，不能者止。'危而不持，颠而不扶，则将焉用彼相矣？且尔言过矣，虎、兕出于柙，龟、玉毁于椟中，

BOOK SIXTEEN

1   (1) The Head of the Chi Family decided to attack Chuan-yü.[1]
(2) Jan Ch'iu and Tzu-lu[2] came to see Master K'ung and said to
him, The Head of the Chi Family has decided to take steps with
regard to Chuan-yü. (3) Master K'ung said, Ch'iu, I fear you
must be held responsible for this crime. (4) Chuan-yü was long
ago appointed by the Former Kings[3] to preside over the sacrifices
to Mount Tung-mêng. Moreover, it lies within the boundaries
of our State, and its ruler is a servant of our own Holy Ground
and Millet. How can such an attack be justified?

(5) Jan Ch'iu said, It is our employer who desires it. Neither of
us two ministers desires it. (6) Master K'ung said, Ch'iu, among
the sayings of Chou Jen[4] there is one which runs: 'He who can
bring his powers into play steps into the ranks;[5] he who cannot,
stays behind.' Of what use to anyone are such counsellors as you,
who see your master tottering, but do not give him a hand, see
him falling, but do not prop him up? (7) Moreover, your plea is a
false one. For if a tiger or wild buffalo escapes from its cage or a
precious ornament of tortoise-shell or jade gets broken in its box,
whose fault is it?[6]

1   A small independent State within the borders of Lu.
2   Who were in the service of the Chi Family.
3   The Chou Emperors.
4   An ancient sage. Further sayings by him are quoted in *Tso Chuan*, Yin
Kung, 6th year, and Chao Kung, 5th year. I fancy he is the same
person as the Ch'ih Jên of the *Shu Ching* (P'an Kêng, Part 1).
5   Military metaphor, here applied to politics.
6   i.e. it is the fault of the person in charge of these things.

是谁之过与?" 冉有曰: "今夫颛臾, 固而近于费。今不取, 后世必为子孙忧。" 孔子曰: "求! 君子疾夫舍曰欲之, 而必为之辞。丘也闻有国有家者, 不患寡而患不均, 不患贫而患不安。盖均无贫, 和无寡, 安无倾。夫如是, 故远人不服, 则修文德以来之。既来之, 则安之。今由与求也, 相夫子, 远人不服而不能来也, 邦分崩离析而不能守也, 而谋动干戈于邦内。吾恐季孙之忧, 不在于颛臾, 而在萧墙之内也。"

(二)

孔子曰: "天下有道, 则礼乐征伐自天子出。天

(8) Jan Ch'iu said, The present situation is this: Chuan-yü is strongly fortified and is close to Pi.[1] If he does not take it now, in days to come it will certainly give trouble to his sons or grandsons. (9) Master K'ung said, Ch'iu, a true gentleman, having once denied that he is in favour of a course, thinks it wrong to make any attempt to condone that course. (10) Concerning the head of a State or Family I have heard the saying:

> He is not concerned lest his people should be poor,
> But only lest what they have should be ill-apportioned.
> He is not concerned lest they should be few,
> But only lest they should be divided against one another.[2]

And indeed, if all is well-apportioned, there will be no poverty; if they are not divided against one another, there will be no lack of men.[3] (1) If such a state of affairs exists, yet the people of far-off lands still do not submit, then the ruler must attract them by enhancing the prestige (te) of his culture; and when they have been duly attracted, he contents them. And where there is contentment there will be no upheavals.

(12) Today with you two, Yu and Ch'iu, acting as counsellors to your master, the people of far lands do not submit to him, and he is not able to attract them. The State itself is divided and tottering, disrupted and cleft, but he can do nothing to save it and is now planning to wield buckler and axe within the borders of his own land. I am afraid that the troubles of the Chi Family are due not to what is happening in Chuan-yü, but to what is going on behind the screen-wall of his own gate.[4]

2   Master K'ung said, When the Way prevails under Heaven all orders concerning ritual, music and punitive expeditions are issued by the Son of Heaven himself. When the Way does not

---

1   The chief castle of the Chi Family.
2   The text of this little poem is slightly corrupt.
3   The words *an wu ch'ing* have become displaced. They belong after *an chih*, 21 characters further on.
4   His own lack of *te* and the fact that he has bad advisers.

下无道，则礼乐征伐自诸侯出。自诸侯出，盖十世希
不失矣。自大夫出，五世希不失矣。陪臣执国命，三
世希不失矣。天下有道，则政不在大夫。天下有道，
则庶人不议。"

（三）

孔子曰：　"禄之去公室，五世矣。政逮于大夫，
四世矣。故夫三桓之子孙微矣。"

（四）

孔子曰：　"益者三友，损者三友。友直，友谅，
友多闻，益矣。友便辟，友善柔，友便佞，损矣。"

（五）

孔子曰：　"益者三乐，损者三乐。乐节礼乐，

prevail, such orders are issued by the feudal princes; and when this happens, it is to be observed that ten generations rarely pass before the dynasty falls. If such orders are issued by State Ministers, five generations rarely pass before they lose their power. When the retainers[1] of great Houses seize a country's commission,[2] three generations rarely pass before they lose their power. When the Way prevails under Heaven, policy is not decided by Ministers; when the Way prevails under Heaven, commoners[3] do not discuss public affairs.

3 Master K'ung said, Power over the exchequer was lost by the Ducal House[4] five generations ago, and government has been in the hands of Ministers[5] for four generations. Small wonder that the descendants of the Three Huan[6] are fast losing their power!

4 Master K'ung said, There are three sorts of friend that are profitable, and three sorts that are harmful. Friendship with the upright, with the true-to-death and with those who have heard much is profitable. Friendship with the obsequious, friendship with those who are good at accommodating their principles, friendship with those who are clever at talk is harmful.

5 Master K'ung said, There are three sorts of pleasure that are profitable, and three sorts of pleasure that are harmful. The pleasure got from the due ordering of ritual and music, the

1 Such as Yang Huo, who seized power in Lu in 505 BC.
2 The *ming* of a State is the charge whereby the Emperor appoints its feudal lord.
3 People not belonging to the Imperial family.
4 Surrendered by the Duke to the Three Families.
5 The heads of the Chi Family. The first three paragraphs of this book seem to form a connected unity. It was under Chi K'ang-tzu (succeeded in 492 BC) that Tzu-lu and Jan Ch'iu were colleagues. If we take paragraph 3 as having been spoken subsequent to 492 BC, the five powerless Dukes must be Ch'êng, Hsiang, Chao, Ting and Ai; and the four Ministers, Chi Wu-tzu, Chi P'ing-tzu, Chi Huan-tzu and Chi K'ang-tzu. But it would be a mistake to try to fit into too strict a chronology sayings that may be purely legendary.
6 The Three Families, Chi, Mêng and Shu.

乐道人之善，乐多贤友，益矣。乐骄乐，乐佚游，乐
宴乐，损矣。”

（六）

　　孔子曰：“侍于君子有三愆：言未及之而言，谓
之躁；言及之而不言，谓之隐；未见颜色而言，谓之
瞽。”

（七）

　　孔子曰：“君子有三戒；少之时，血气未定，戒
之在色；及其壮也，血气方刚，戒之在斗；及其老也，
血气既衰，戒之在得。”

（八）

　　孔子曰：“君子有三畏：畏天命，畏大人，畏圣
人之言。小人不知天命而不畏也，狎大人，侮圣人之
言。”

（九）

　　孔子曰：“生而知之者，上也。学而知之者，次
也。困而学之，又其次也。困而不学，民斯为下矣。”

pleasure got from discussing the good points in the conduct of others, the pleasure of having many wise friends is profitable. But pleasure got from profligate enjoyments, pleasure got from idle gadding about, pleasure got from comfort and ease is harmful.

6　Master K'ung said, There are three mistakes that are liable to be made when waiting upon a gentleman. To speak before being called upon to do so; this is called forwardness. Not to speak when called upon to do so; this is called secretiveness. To speak without first noting the expression of his face; this is called 'blindness'.[1]

7　Master K'ung said, There are three things against which a gentleman is on his guard. In his youth, before his blood and vital humours[2] have settled down, he is on his guard against lust. Having reached his prime, when the blood and vital humours have finally hardened, he is on his guard against strife. Having reached old age, when the blood and vital humours are already decaying, he is on his guard against avarice.

8　Master K'ung said, There are three things that a gentleman fears: he fears the will of Heaven, he fears great men,[3] he fears the words of the Divine Sages. The small man does not know the will of Heaven and so does not fear it. He treats great men with contempt, and scoffs at the words of the Divine Sages.

9　Master K'ung said, Highest are those who are born wise. Next are those who become wise by learning. After them come those who have to toil painfully in order to acquire learning. Finally, to the lowest class of the common people belong those who toil painfully without ever managing to learn.

1　cf. *Hsün Tzu*, P'ien, 1, end.
2　The physiological theories which underlie this paragraph are, I suspect, considerably posterior to Confucius.
3　*Ta-jen* means (1) giants; (2) ministers, persons in authority; (3) morally great, as in *Mencius*, IV, B, 6; 11 and 12, etc. Probably the meaning here is 'morally great'; that is to say, people like Confucius himself.

（十）

孔子曰：　"子有九思：视思明，听思聪，色思温，貌思恭，言思忠，事思敬，疑思问，忿思难，见得思义。"

（十一）

孔子曰：　"见善如不及，见不善如探汤，吾见其人矣，吾闻其语矣。隐居以求其志，行义以达其道，吾闻其语矣，未见其人也。"

（十二）

齐景公有马千驷，死之日，民无德而称焉。伯夷、叔齐饿于首阳之下，民到于今称之。其斯之谓与?

（十三）

陈亢问于伯鱼曰：　"子亦有异闻乎?"　对曰：　"未

10 Master K'ung said, The gentleman has nine cares. In seeing he is careful to see clearly, in hearing he is careful to hear distinctly, in his looks he is careful to bc kindly; in his manner to be respectful, in his words to be loyal, in his work to be diligent. When in doubt he is careful to ask for information; when angry he has a care for the consequences, and when he sees a chance of gain, he thinks carefully whether the pursuit of it would be consonant with the Right.

11, 12 Master K'ung said, 'When they see what is good, they grasp at it as though they feared it would elude them. When they see what is not good, they test it cautiously, as though putting a finger into hot water.' I have heard this saying; I have even seen such men.[1] 'It is by dwelling in seclusion that they seek the fulfilment of their aims; it is by deeds of righteousness that they extend the influence of their Way.' I have heard this saying; but I have never seen such men. 'Duke Ching of Ch'i had a thousand teams of horses; but on the day of his death the people could think of no good deed for which to praise him.[2] Po I and Shu Ch'i[3] starved at[4] the foot of Mount Shou-yang; yet the people sing their praises down to this very day.' Does not this saying illustrate the other?[5]

13 Tzu-ch'in[6] questioned Po Yü[7] saying, As his son[8] you must after

---

1 These two clauses are accidentally inverted in the original.

2 This is clearly the same formula as VIII, 1 (end), where, however, it is used in praise and not, as here, in condemnation.

3 See V, 22.

4 This form of the preposition, which occurs twice here but nowhere else in the *Analects*, marks the passage as a quotation from some other text. Moreover, the passage is closed by a formula (*ch'i ssu chih wei*) which regularly follows quotations.

5 i.e. are not Po I and Shu Ch'i examples of people who dwelt in seclusion to fulfil their aims, by deeds of righteousness extended the influence of the Way?

6 See I, 10.

7 Confucius's son; see XI, 7.

8 *Tzu* here means 'son' and not 'you, my master'.

也。尝独立，鲤趋而过庭。曰：'学诗乎？'对曰：'未也。' '不学诗，无以言。'鲤退而学诗。他日，又独立，鲤趋而过庭。曰：'学礼乎？'对曰：'未也。' '不学礼，无以立。'鲤退而学礼。闻斯二矣。"陈亢退而喜，曰："问一得三，闻诗，闻礼，又闻君子之远其子也。"

(十四)

邦君之妻，君称之曰夫人，夫人自称曰小童，邦人称之曰君夫人，称诸异邦曰寡小君，异邦人称之亦曰君夫人。

all surely have heard something different from what the rest of us hear. Po Yü replied saying, No. Once when he was standing alone and I was hurrying[1] past him across the courtyard, he said, Have you studied the *Songs*? I replied saying, No. (He said) If you do not study the *Songs*, you will find yourself at a loss in conversation. So I retired and studied the *Songs*. Another day he was again standing alone, and as I hurried across the courtyard, he said, Have you studied the rituals? I replied saying, No. (He said) If you do not study the rituals, you will find yourself at a loss how to take your stand.[2] So I retired and studied the rituals. These two things I heard from him.

Tzu-ch'in came away delighted, saying, I asked about one point, but got information about three. I learnt about the *Songs*, about the rituals, and also learnt that a gentleman keeps his son at a distance.[3]

14 The wife of the ruler of a State is referred to by the ruler as 'That person'. She refers to herself as Little Boy. The people of the country call her 'That person of the Prince's'. When speaking of her to people of another State the ruler calls her 'This lonely one's little prince'. But people of another State likewise call her 'That person of the Prince's'.[4]

1 As a sign of respect.
2 On public occasions.
3 The reasons why a gentleman must not teach his own son are discussed in *Mencius*, IV, A, 16. There is a definite ritual severance between father and son. A father may not carry his son in his arms. A son may not, when sacrifice is being made to his deceased father, act as the 'medium' into whom the spirit of the deceased passes. See *Li Chi*, I, fol. 5.
4 This paragraph is a passage on etiquette from some old handbook of ritual, and was probably inserted here merely because it was found along with the manuscript of this *p'ien* (chapter). See additional notes, and cf. *Li Chi*, II, fol. 3.

阳货第十七

(一)

阳货欲见孔子，孔子不见，归孔子豚。孔子时其亡也，而往拜之，遇诸涂。谓孔子曰："来 予与尔言。"曰："怀其宝而迷其邦，可谓仁乎?"曰："不可。""好从事而亟失时，可谓智乎?"曰："不可。""日月逝矣，岁不我与。"孔子曰："诺，吾将仕矣。"

(二)

子曰："性相近也，习相远也。"

(三)

子曰："唯上智与下愚不移。"

BOOK SEVENTEEN

1   Yang Huo[1] wanted to see Master K'ung; but Master K'ung would not see him. He sent Master K'ung a sucking pig. Master K'ung, choosing a time when he knew Yang Huo would not be at home, went to tender acknowledgment; but met him in the road. He spoke to Master K'ung, saying, Come here, I have something to say to you. What he said was, Can one who hides his jewel[2] in his bosom and lets his country continue to go astray be called Good? Certainly not. Can one who longs to take part in affairs, yet time after time misses the opportunity to do so — can such a one be called wise? Certainly not.[3] The days and months go by, the years do not wait upon our bidding. Master K'ung said, All right;[4] I am going to serve.

2   The Master said, By nature, near together; by practice far apart.[5]

3   The Master said, It is only the very wisest and the very stupidest who cannot change.

1   See XVI, 2, note. For the anecdote, cf. *Mencius*, III, B, 7.

2   i.e. his talents. cf. XV, 6.

3   Yang Huo answers his own rhetorical questions, a common formula in Chinese.

4   The form of assent Confucius uses implies reluctance. This story, like those in Books XVIII and XIII, certainly originated in non-Confucian circles and comes from the same sort of source as the Confucius Anecdotes in the Taoist works *Chuang Tzu* and *Lieh Tzu*.

5   This proverbial saying has wide possibilities of application. It here presumably means that goodness is a matter of training and application and not an inborn quality.

（四）

子之武城，闻弦歌之声。夫子莞尔而笑曰："割鸡焉用牛刀?"子游对曰："昔者偃也闻诸夫子曰：'君子学道则爱人，小人学道则易使也。'"子曰："二三子，偃之言是也，前言戏之耳。"

（五）

公山弗扰以费畔，召，子欲往。子路不悦，曰："末之也已，何必公山氏之之也?"子曰："夫召我者，而岂徒哉? 如有用我者，吾其为东周乎?"

（六）

子张问仁于孔子。孔子曰："能行五者于天下，为仁矣。""请问之。"曰："恭，宽，信，敏，惠。恭则不侮，宽则得众，信则人任焉，敏则有功，惠则

4   When the Master went to the walled town of Wu,[1] he heard the
     sound of stringed instruments and singing. Our Master said with
     a gentle smile, 'To kill a chicken one does not use an ox-
     cleaver.'[2] Tzu-yu replied saying, I remember once hearing you
     say, 'A gentleman who has studied the Way will be all the
     tenderer towards his fellow-men; a commoner who has studied
     the Way will be all the easier to employ.' The Master said, My
     disciples, what he says is quite true. What I said just now was
     only meant as a joke.

5   Kung-shan Fu-jao,[3] when he was holding the castle of Pi in
     revolt (against the Chi Family), sent for the Master, who would
     have liked to go; but Tzu-lu did not approve of this and said to
     the Master, After having refused in so many cases, why go to
     Kung-shan of all people? The Master said, It cannot be for
     nothing[4] that he has sent for me. If anyone were to use me, I
     believe I could make a 'Chou in the east'.[5]

6   Tzu-chang asked Master K'ung about Goodness. Master K'ung
     said, He who could put the Five into practice everywhere under
     Heaven would be Good. Tzu-chang begged to hear what these
     were. The Master said, Courtesy, breadth, good faith, diligence
     and clemency. 'He who is courteous is not scorned, he who is
     broad wins the multitude, he who is of good faith is trusted by

1   Where Tzu-yu was in command. See VI, 12.
2   A saying of proverbial type meaning, in effect, that in teaching music to
     the inhabitants of this small town Tzu-yu is 'casting pearls before
     swine'. The proverb may well have had a second, balancing clause,
     here alluded to, but not expressed; such as, 'To teach commoners one
     does not use a zithern.'
3   Warden of Pi, the chief stronghold of the Chi Family. He revolted
     in 502 BC, but in 498 BC he fled to Ch'i and later to Wu where he is
     said to have plotted, in a spirit of petty revenge, against his native State
     of Lu.
4   Confucius believes that Kung-shan intends to restore the Duke to his
     rightful powers.
5   Create a second Golden Age, comparable to the early days of the Chou
     dynasty.

足以使人。"

(七)

佛肸召，子欲往。子路曰："昔者由也闻诸夫子曰：'亲于其身为不善者，君子不入也。'佛肸以中牟畔，子之往也，如之何?"子曰："然，有是言也。不曰坚乎，磨而不磷；不曰白乎，涅而不缁。吾岂匏瓜也哉? 焉能系而不食!"

(八)

子曰："由也，汝闻六言六蔽矣乎?"对曰："未也。""居! 吾语汝。好仁不好学，其蔽也愚；好知不好学，其蔽也荡；好信不好学，其蔽也贼；好直不好学，其蔽也绞；好勇不好学，其蔽也乱；好刚不好学，其蔽也狂。"

the people, he who is diligent succeeds in all he undertakes, he who is clement can get service from the people.'[1]

7   Pi Hsi[2] summoned the Master, and he would have liked to go. But Tzu-lu said, I remember your once saying, 'Into the house of one who is in his own person doing what is evil, the gentleman will not enter.' Pi Hsi is holding Chung-mou[3] in revolt. How can you think of going to him? The Master said, It is true that there is such a saying. But is it not also said that there are things 'So hard that no grinding will ever wear them down', that there are things 'So white that no steeping will ever make them black'? Am I indeed to be forever like the bitter gourd that is only fit to hang up,[4] but not to eat?[5]

8   The Master said, Yu, have you ever been told of the Six Sayings about the Six Degenerations? Tzu-lu replied, No, never. (The Master said) Come, then; I will tell you. Love of Goodness without love of learning[6] degenerates into silliness. Love of wisdom without love of learning degenerates into utter lack of principle. Love of keeping promises without love of learning degenerates into villainy.[7] Love of uprightness without love of learning[8] degenerates into harshness. Love of courage without love of learning degenerates into turbulence.[9] Love of courage without love of learning degenerates into mere recklessness.

1   This is almost certainly a quotation from some text of the *Shu Ching*. cf. XX, 1, where most of it reappears.
2   A Chin officer.
3   A town in Wei, captured by the Chin (in 490?).
4   Till it is dry and can be used as a vessel.
5   Play on two senses of *shih* (1) to eat; (2) to get a salary, an official post.
6   i.e. learning the Way of the ancients.
7   i.e. keeping regrettable pacts and promises to the detriment of *i* (what is right under the circumstances).
8   Like that of Upright Kung, XIII, 18.
9   The tendency to fling oneself into any revolutions or upheavals that are going on in the world around one.

（九）

子曰：“小子何莫学夫诗？诗可以兴，可以观，可以群，可以怨，迩之事父，远之事君，多识于鸟兽草木之名。”

（十）

子谓伯鱼曰：“女为《周南》、《召南》矣乎？人而不为《周南》、《召南》，其犹正墙面而立也与！”

（十一）

子曰：“礼云礼云，玉帛云乎哉？乐云乐云，钟鼓云乎哉？”

（十二）

子曰：“色厉而内荏，譬诸小人，其犹穿窬之盗也与？”

（十三）

子曰：“乡愿，德之贼也。”

（十四）

子曰：“道听而涂说，德之弃也。”

（十五）

子曰：“鄙夫可与事君也与哉！其未得之也，患得之。既得之，患失之。苟患失之，无所不至矣。”

9   The Master said, Little ones, Why is it that none of you stu[dy the]
     Songs? For the *Songs* will help you to incite people's emotions, to
     observe their feelings, to keep company, to express your
     grievances. They may be used at home in the service of one's
     father; abroad, in the service of one's prince.[1] Moreover, they
     will widen your acquaintance with the names[2] of birds, beasts,
     plants and trees.

10   The Master addressed Po Yü[3] saying, Have you done the *Chou
     Nan* and the *Shao Nan*[4] yet? He who has not even done the
     Chou Nan and the *Shao Nan* is as though he stood with his face
     pressed against a wall!

11   The Master said, Ritual, ritual! Does it mean no more than
     presents of jade and silk?[5] Music, music! Does it mean no more
     than bells and drums?

12   The Master said, To assume an outward air of fierceness when
     inwardly trembling is (to take a comparison from low walks of
     life) as dishonest as to sneak into places where one has no right to
     be, by boring a hole or climbing through a gap.

13   The Master said, The 'honest villager' spoils[6] true virtue (*te*).

14   The Master said, To tell in the lane what you have heard on the
     highroad is to throw merit (*te*) away.

15   The Master said, How could one ever possibly serve one's prince
     alongside of such low-down creatures? Before they have got
     office, they think about nothing but how to get it; and when
     they have got it, all they care about is to avoid losing it. And so
     soon as they see themselves in the slightest danger of losing it,
     there is no length to which they will not go.

1   For the uses of the *Songs* here inculcated, see *The Book of Songs*, p 335.
2   i.e. the 'correct names', the names in the ancient Court dialect used in
     ritual, as opposed to the local names.
3   Son of Confucius. See XVI, 13.
4   The first two books of the *Songs*.
5   cf. *Hsün Tzu*, P'ien, 27, fol. 1.
6   As we should say 'Spoils the market for . . .' For a long discussion of
     this saying, see *Mencius*, VII, B, 37.

（十六）

子曰：“古者民有三疾，今也或是之亡也。古之狂也肆，今之狂也荡；古之矜也廉，今之矜也忿戾；古之愚也直，今之愚也诈而已矣。”

（十七）

子曰：“巧言令色，鲜矣仁。”

（十八）

子曰：“恶紫之夺朱也，恶郑声之乱雅乐也，恶利口之覆邦家者。”

（十九）

子曰：“予欲无言。”子贡曰：“子如不言，则小子何述焉？”子曰：“天何言哉？四时行焉，百物生焉，天何言哉？”

（二十）

孺悲欲见孔子，孔子辞以疾。将命者出户，取瑟而歌，使之闻之。

16 In old days the common people had three faults, part[1] of which
they have now lost. In old days the impetuous were merely
impatient of small restraints; now they are utterly insubordinate.
In old days the proud were stiff and formal; now they are touchy
and quarrelsome. In old days simpletons were at any rate
straightforward; but now 'simple-mindedness' exists only as a
device of the impostor.

17 The Master said, Clever talk and a pretentious manner are
seldom found in the Good.[2]

18 The Master said, I hate to see roan killing red, I hate to see the
tunes of Chêng[3] corrupting Court music, I hate to see sharp
mouths overturning kingdoms and clans.

19 The Master said, I would much rather not have to talk. Tzu-
kung said, If our Master did not talk, what should we little ones
have to hand down about him? The Master said, Heaven does
not speak; yet the four seasons run their course thereby,[4] the
hundred creatures, each after its kind, are born thereby. Heaven
does no speaking!

20 Ju Pei[5] wanted to see Master K'ung. Master K'ung excused
himself on the ground of ill-health. But when the man who had
brought the message was going out through the door he took up
his zithern and sang, taking good care that the messenger should
hear.

---

1   What follows is a paradox, for we expect to hear that the people have
     improved; whereas it turns out that the 'lost parts' were redeeming
     features.
2   Identical with I, 3.
3   See XV, 10. cf. also *Mencius*, VII, B, 37.
4   By command of Heaven.
5   Of whom practically nothing is known. He had evidently disgraced
     himself.

(二十一)

宰我问三年之丧：“期已久矣。君子三年不为礼，礼必坏；三年不为乐，乐必崩。旧谷既没，新谷既升，钻燧改火，期可已矣。”子曰：“食夫稻，衣夫锦，于女安乎？”曰：“安。”“女安则为之。夫君子之居丧，食旨不甘，闻乐不乐，居处不安，故不为也。今女安则为之。”宰我出。曰：“予之不仁也！子生三年，然后免于父母之怀。夫三年之丧，天下之通丧也。予也，有三年之爱于其父母乎？”

21 Tsai Yü[1] asked about the three years' mourning,[2] and said he thought a year would be quite long enough: 'If gentlemen suspend their practice of the rites[3] for three years, the rites will certainly decay; if for three years they make no music, music will certainly be destroyed.'[4] (In a year) the old crops have already vanished, the new crops have come up, the whirling drills have made new fire.[5] Surely a year would be enough?

The Master said, Would you then (after a year) feel at ease in eating good rice and wearing silk brocades? Tsai Yü said, Quite at ease. (The Master said) If you would really feel at ease, then do so. But when a true gentleman is in mourning, if he eats dainties, he does not relish them, if he hears music, it does not please him, if he sits in his ordinary seat, he is not comfortable. That is why he abstains from these things. But if you would really feel at ease, there is no need for you to abstain.

When Tsai Yü had gone out, the Master said, How inhuman[6] Yü is! Only when a child is three years old does it leave its parents' arms. The three years' mourning is the universal mourning everywhere under Heaven.[7] And Yü – was he not the darling of his father and mother for three years?

1 See V, 9.

2 For parents. Three years is often interpreted as meaning 'into the third year', i.e. 25 months.

3 The mourning for parents entailed complete suspension of all ordinary activities.

4 A traditional saying. cf. *Shih Chi*, Ch. 28, beginning.

5 The ritualists describe four 'fire-changing' rites, one for each season, the new fire being in each case kindled on the wood of a tree appropriate to the season. But perhaps the only actual 'fire-changing', when all fires were put out and after three days rekindled from a new ritually-obtained flame, was in the spring. See *Hou Han Shu*, LXI, fol. 6, recto and *Chou Li*, Ch. 57 (commentary).

6 *Jen* is here used in its later sense, 'possessing human feelings', 'kind'. This chapter shows many signs of late date.

7 The whole object of this paragraph is to claim Confucius as a supporter of the three years' mourning. This custom was certainly far from being 'universal', and was probably not ancient. cf. *Mencius* III, A, 3, where the people of Têng protest that even in Lu 'the former princes none of them practised it'.

(二十二)

子曰：　"饱食终日，无所用心，难矣哉！不有博弈者乎？为之犹贤乎已。"

(二十三)

子路曰：　"君子尚勇乎？"子曰：　"君子义以为上。君子有勇而无义为乱，小人有勇而无义为盗。"

(二十四)

子贡曰：　"君子亦有恶乎？"子曰：　"有恶。恶称人之恶者，恶居下流而讪上者，恶勇而无礼者，恶果敢而窒者。"曰：　"赐也亦有恶乎？""恶徼以为智者，恶不逊以为勇者，恶讦以为直者。"

(二十五)

子曰：　"唯女子与小人为难养也，近之则不逊，远之则怨。"

(二十六)

子曰：　"年四十而见恶焉，其终也已。"

22 The Master said, Those who do nothing all day but cram themselves with food and never use their minds are difficult. Are there not games such as draughts?[2] To play them would surely be better than doing nothing at all.

23 Tzu-lu said, Is courage to be prized by a gentleman? The Master said, A gentleman gives the first place to Right. If a gentleman has courage but neglects Right, he becomes turbulent. If a small man has courage but neglects Right, he becomes a thief.

24 Tzu-kung said, Surely even the gentleman must have his hatreds. The Master said, He has his hatreds. He hates those who point out what is hateful in others.[3] He hates those who dwelling in low estate[4] revile all who are above them. He hates those who love deeds of daring but neglect ritual. He hates those who are active and venturesome, but are violent in temper. I suppose you also have your hatreds? Tzu-kung said,[5] I hate those who mistake cunning for wisdom. I hate those who mistake insubordination for courage. I hate those who mistake tale-bearing for honesty.

25 The Master said, Women and people of low birth are very hard to deal with. If you are friendly with them, they get out of hand, and if you keep your distance, they resent it.[6]

26 The Master said, One who has reached the age of forty and is still disliked will be so till the end.

---

1 cf. XV, 16.
2 For draughts, see *Tso Chuan*, Duke Hsiang, 25th year, end. It no doubt resembled the current game of *wei-ch'i*. I think *po* (cognate with *po* 'to strike', cf. Japanese *utsu*, 'to strike', i.e. make a move in board-games) is to be taken with *i* and is not the name of a separate game.
3 cf. *Kuan Tzu*, P'ien, 66, end.
4 *liu* has been wrongly inserted here on the analogy of XIX, 20.
5 This 'said' has accidentally been transferred to the clause above.
6 Like Liu Pao-nan, I take *nü-tzu* in its ordinary sense of 'women' as opposed to 'men', and *hsiao jen* in its ordinary sense of 'cads' as opposed to 'gentlemen'. The standard interpreters soften the saying by making it apply to 'maids and valets'.

微子第十八

(一)

微子去之，箕子为之奴，比干谏而死。孔子曰：
"殷有三仁焉。"

(二)

柳下惠为士师，三黜。人曰："子未可以去乎?"
曰："直道而事人，焉往而不三黜? 枉道而事人，何
必去父母之邦?"

(三)

齐景公待孔子曰："若季氏，则吾不能，以季孟
之间待之。"曰："吾老矣，不能用也。"孔子行。

BOOK EIGHTEEN

1   'The lord of Wei fled from him,[1] the lord of Chi suffered slavery at his hands, Pi Kan rebuked him and was slain.' Master K'ung said, In them the Yin had three Good men.

2   When Liu-hsia Hui[2] was Leader of the Knights,[3] he was three times dismissed. People said to him, Surely you would do well to seek service elsewhere? He said, If I continue to serve men in honest ways, where can I go and not be three times dismissed? If, on the other hand, I am willing to serve men by crooked ways, what need is there for me to leave the land of my father and mother?

3   Duke Ching of Ch'i received Master K'ung; he said, To treat him on an equality with the head of the Chi Family is impossible. I will receive him as though he ranked between the head of the Chi and the head of the Mêng. (At the interview) he said, I am old and have no use for you. Whereupon Master K'ung left (the land of Ch'i).[4]

1   i.e. from the tyrant Chou, last sovereign of the Yin dynasty. The lord of Wei was his step-brother. The lord of Chi and Pi Kan were his uncles.
2   See XV, 13.
3   A comparatively humble post. Its occupant was chiefly concerned with criminal cases.
4   Book XVIII is wholly legendary in content. The Confucius who ranked above the head of the Mêng family is already well on the way towards apotheosis.

（四）

齐人归女乐，季桓子受之，三日不朝，孔子行。

（五）

楚狂接舆歌而过孔子，曰：　"风兮，风兮！何德之衰？往者不可谏，来者犹可追。已而，已而！今之从政者殆而。"孔子下，欲与之言。趋而避之，不得与之言。

（六）

长沮、桀溺耦而耕，孔子过之，使子路问津焉。长沮曰：　"夫执舆者为谁？"子路曰：　"为孔丘。"曰：　"是鲁孔丘与？"曰：　"是也。"曰：　"是知津矣。"问于桀溺。桀溺曰：　"子为谁？"曰：　"为仲由。"曰：　"是鲁孔丘之徒与？"对曰：　"然。"曰：　"滔滔者天

4 The people of Ch'i sent to Lu a present of female musicians,[1] and Chi Huan-tzu[2] accepted them. For three days no Court was held, whereupon Master K'ung left Lu.

5 Chieh Yü,[3] the madman of Ch'u, came past Master K'ung, singing as he went:

> Oh phoenix, phoenix
> How dwindled is your power!
> As to the past, reproof is idle,
> But the future may yet be remedied.
> Desist, desist!
> Great in these days is the peril of those who fill office.

Master K'ung got down,[4] desiring to speak with him; but the madman hastened his step and got away, so that Master K'ung did not succeed in speaking to him.

6 Ch'ang-chü and Chieh-ni[5] were working as plough-mates together. Master K'ung, happening to pass that way, told Tzu-lu to go and ask them where the river could be forded. Ch'ang-chü said, Who is it for whom you are driving? Tzu-lu said, For K'ung Ch'iu. He said, What, K'ung Ch'iu of Lu? Tzu-lu said, Yes, he. Ch'ang-chü said, In that case he already knows where the ford is.[6] Tzu-lu then asked Chieh-ni. Chieh-ni said, Who are you? He said, I am Tzu-lu. Chien-ni said, You are a follower of K'ung Ch'iu of Lu, are you not? He said, That is so. Chieh-ni said, Under Heaven there is none that is not swept along by the

1 In order to weaken the power of the government. A common folk-lore theme.

2 The father of Chi K'ang-tzu; died 492 BC. This is the only passage in the *Analects* where he is directly mentioned.

3 See *Chuang Tzu*, IV, 8, where this typically Taoist, anti-Confucian story is told in a slightly longer form. For the 'madman', see also *Chuang Tzu*, I, 4 and VII, 2, *Hsin Hsü*, III. *Han Fei Tzu*, P'ien, 20. *Chan Kuo T'sê*, Ch'in stories, Pt. II.

4 From his carriage.

5 The names recall in their formation those of the fictitious personages in *Chuang Tzu* and *Lieh Tzu*.

6 Or should do; for he claims to be a Sage.

下皆是也，而谁以易之？且而与其从避人之士也，岂若
从避世之士哉！”耰而不辍。子路行，以告。夫子怃然
曰：“鸟兽不可与同群，吾非斯人之徒与而谁与？天下
有道，丘不与易也。”

(七)

　　子路从而后，遇丈人，以杖荷蓧。子路问曰：“子
见夫子乎？”丈人曰：“四体不勤，五谷不分，孰为夫
子？”植其杖而芸。子路拱而立。止子路宿，杀鸡为黍
而食之，见其二子焉。明日，子路行，以告。子曰：“隐

same flood. Such is the world and who can change it? As for you, instead of following one who flees from this man and that, you would do better to follow one who shuns this whole generation of men. And with that he went on covering the seed.

Tzu-lu went and told his master, who said ruefully, One cannot herd with birds and beasts. If I am not to be a man among other men, then what am I to be?[1] If the Way prevailed under Heaven, I should not be trying to alter things.

7   Once when Tzu-lu was following (the Master) he fell behind and met an old man carrying a basket[2] slung over his staff. Tzu-lu asked him, saying, Sir, have you seen my master? The old man said, You who

> With your four limbs do not toil,
> Who do not sift the five grains,[3]

who is your master? And with that he planted his staff in the ground and began weeding, while Tzu-lu stood by with his hands pressed together.[4]

He kept Tzu-lu for the night, killed a fowl, prepared a dish of millet for his supper and introduced him to his two sons. Tzu-lu said, It is not right to refuse to serve one's country. The laws of age and youth may not be set aside. And how can it be right for a man to set aside the duty that binds minister to prince, or in his desire to maintain his own integrity, to subvert the Great Relationship?[5] A gentleman's service to his country consists in doing such right as he can. That the Way does not prevail, he knows well enough beforehand.

Next day[6] Tzu-lu went on his way and reported what had

1   I think the second *yü*, like the first, is interrogative.   2   cf. XIV, 20.
3   Who would not know how to choose the right seed for sowing. The five kinds of grain are rice, two kinds of millet, wheat and pulse.
4   The palms pressed together in an attitude of respect.
5   This is the only book in the *Analects* in which the term *lun* (relationship) which figures so prominently in later Confucianism, makes its appearance.
6   In the original this clause down to 'gone away' follows the words 'his two sons'. This makes the whole story run very awkwardly; see T.T. 2036. The clauses have certainly become accidentally inverted.

者也。”使子路反见之，至，则行矣。子路曰：“不仕无义。长幼之节，不可废也；君臣之义，如之何其可废之?欲洁其身，而乱大伦。君子之仕也，行其义也。道之不行，已知之矣。”

(八)

逸民：伯夷、叔齐、虞仲、夷逸、朱张、柳下惠、少连。子曰：“不降其志，不辱其身，伯夷、叔齐与!”谓柳下惠、少连：“降志辱身矣，言中伦，行中虑，其斯而已矣。”谓虞仲、夷逸：“隐居放言，身中清，废中权。我则异于是，无可无不可。”

(九)

大师挚适齐，亚饭干适楚，三饭缭适蔡，四饭缺

happened. The Master said, He is a recluse, and told Tzu-lu to go back and visit him again. But on arriving at the place he found that the old man had gone away.[1]

8 Subjects whose services were lost to the State: Po I, Shu Ch'i,[2] Yü Chung,[3] I I, Chu Chang,[4] Liu-hsia Hui, Shao Lien.[5] The Master said, Those of them who 'would neither abate their high resolve nor bring humiliation upon themselves' were, I suppose, Po I and Shu Ch'i. It means that[6] Liu-hsia Hui and Shao Lien did abate their high resolve and bring humiliation upon themselves. 'Their words were consonant with the Relationships, their deeds were consonant with prudence; this and no more,' means that Yü Chung and I I, on the contrary, lived in seclusion and refrained from comment. They secured personal integrity; and when set aside maintained due balance.[7] As for me, I am different from any of these. I have no 'thou shalt' or 'thou shalt not'.

9 The Chief Musician Chih[8] betook himself to Ch'i; Kan, the leader of the band at the second meal,[9] betook himself to Ch'u, Liao (leader of the band at the third meal) went to Ts'ai, and

1 Fearing that Confucius might recommend him for public service? Compare the very similar story, *Chuang Tzu*, XXV, 5.

2 For Po I and Shu Ch'i, see V, 22.

3 Brother of T'ai Po, VIII, 1.

4 I I and Chu Chang are unknown. I suspect that Chu Chang at any rate is not a proper name at all, but a corruption of part of the sentence. This was clearly suspected by Lu Tê-ming (*c*.AD 600).

5 For Liu-hsia Hui, see XV, 13. Shao-lien is said to have been an 'eastern barbarian'.

6 Confucius seems here to be commenting on some text which is unknown to us.

7 This whole paragraph is certainly corrupt. Liu-hsia Hui hung on to office despite every rebuff, and cannot be counted as a 'lost subject'. After the name of I I some phrase must have followed meaning, 'those who concealed their discontent', or the like.

8 cf. VIII, 15. It is natural to suppose that this migration took place when Duke Chao of Lu fled to Ch'i in 517 BC.

9 Or 'at the second course'.

适秦。鼓方叔人于河，播鼗武入于汉，少师阳、击磬襄
入于海。

(十)

周公谓鲁公曰： "君子不施其亲，不使大臣怨乎
不以。故旧无大故，则不弃也。无求备于一人。"

(十一)

周有八士：伯达、伯适、仲突、仲忽、叔夜、叔
夏、季随、季骑。

Ch'üeh (leader of the band at the fourth meal) went to Ch'in. The big drummer Fang Shu went within [1] the River, the kettle-drummer Wu went within the River Han, the Minor Musician Yang and Hsiang, the player of the stone-chimes, went within the sea.[2]

10   The Duke of Chou addressed the Duke of Lu,[3] saying: A gentleman never discards[4] his kinsmen; nor does he ever give occasion to his chief retainers to chafe at not being used. None who have been long in his service does he ever dismiss without grave cause. He does not expect one man to be capable of everything.[5]

11   Chou had its Eight Knights:

Elder-brother Ta	(d'ât)
Elder-brother Kua	(g'uât)
Middle-brother T'u	(t'ut)
Middle-brother Hu	(hut)
Younger-brother Yeh	(zia)
Younger-brother Hsia	(g'a)
Youngest-brother Sui	(d'uâ)
Youngest-brother Kua	(Kuâ)[6]

1   i.e. to the north of.
2   to an island. This paragraph and the two which follow it are stray fragments arbitrarily inserted at the end of the Book. cf. the terminations of Books X and XVI.   3   His son.
4   The original sense of the maxim may have been 'never reserves all his largesses for his own kinsmen'.   5   cf. XIII, 25.
6   A sign that a country had reached the maximum of plenty and fertility was that one woman should bear four pairs of twins. cf. the similar set of twins mentioned in Tsang Wên Chung's great discourse, *Tso Chuan*, Duke Wên, 18th year. The present set is unknown elsewhere, and commentators cannot decide in what reign the happy phenomenon took place. I give the names in their approximate ancient pronunciation, to show that they form a sort of jingle. 'The names go in pairs, as becomes those of twins,' says Huang K'an. For the pronunciation of the last name I follow Lu Tê-ming.

子张第十九

(一)

子张曰："士见危致命，见得思义，祭思敬，丧思哀，其可已矣。"

(二)

子张曰："执德不弘，信道不笃，焉能为有？焉能为亡？"

(三)

子夏之门人问交于子张。子张曰："子夏云何？"对曰："子夏曰：'可者与之，其不可者拒之。'"子张曰："异乎吾所闻。君子尊贤而容众，嘉善而矜

BOOK NINETEEN

1   Tzu-chang said, A knight who confronted with danger is ready to lay down his life, who confronted with the chance of gain thinks first of right, who judges sacrifice by the degree of reverence shown and mourning by the degree of grief [1] – such a one is all that can be desired.

2   Tzu-chang said, He who sides with moral force (*te*) but only to a limited extent,[2] who believes in the Way, but without conviction – how can one count him as with us, how can one count him as not with us?

3   The disciples of Tzu-hsia asked Tzu-chang about intercourse with others. Tzu-chang said, What does Tzu-hsia tell you? He replied saying, Tzu-hsia says:

> Go with those with whom it is proper to go;
> Keep at a distance those whom it is proper to keep at a distance.

Tzu-chang said, That is different from what I have been told:

> A gentleman reverences those that excel, but 'finds room'[3] for all;
> He commends the good and pities the incapable.

1   And not by the elaborateness of the ceremonies. For the first part of the saying, cf. XIV, 13.
2   Saying for example that *te* has its uses, but that the ultimate appeal must always be to physical compulsion.
3   i.e. tolerates.

不能。我之大贤与，于人何所不容？我之不贤与，人将
拒我，如之何其拒人也？"

(四)

　　子夏曰："虽小道，必有可观者焉，致远恐泥，
是以君子不为也。"

(五)

　　子夏曰："日知其所亡，月无忘其所能，可谓好
学也已矣。"

(六)

　　子夏曰："博学而笃志，切问而近思，仁在其中
矣。"

(七)

　　子夏曰："百工居肆以成其事，君子学以致其道。"

(八)

　　子夏曰："小人之过也必文。"

Do I myself greatly excel others? In that case I shall certainly find room for everyone. Am I myself inferior to others? In that case, it would be others who would keep me at a distance. So that the question of keeping others at a distance does not arise.[1]

4 Tzu-hsia said, Even the minor walks[2] (of knowledge) have an importance of their own. But if pursued too far they tend to prove a hindrance; for which reason a gentleman does not cultivate them.

5 Tzu-hsia said, He who from day to day is conscious of what he still lacks, and from month to month never forgets what he has already learnt, may indeed be called a true lover of learning.

6 Tzu-hsia said,

> One who studies widely and with set purpose,
> Who questions earnestly, then thinks for himself about
>   what he has heard

– such a one will incidentally[3] achieve Goodness.

7 Tzu-hsia said, Just as the hundred[4] apprentices must live in workshops to perfect themselves in their craft, so the gentleman studies, that he may improve himself in the Way.

8 Tzu-hsia said, When the small man goes wrong, it is always on the side of over-elaboration.[5]

---

1 Literally, what becomes of that (*ch'i* in such usages corresponds to the Latin *iste*) 'keeping others at a distance' of yours?
2 Such as agriculture, medicine, etc. The idea that specialised knowledge is incompatible with true gentility prevailed in England till well towards the close of the nineteenth century.
3 cf. II, 18; VII, 15; XIII, 18 and XV, 21.
4 i.e. all the different sorts of . . .
5 Lu Tê-ming does not gloss this character, and therefore presumably read *wên* in its ordinary pronunciation. I see no reason to read it in the 'departing tone', with the meaning 'gloss over', 'make excuses'. The sole authority for the usual interpretation is the pseudo K'ung An-kuo.

（九）

子夏曰："君子有三变：望之俨然，即之也温，听其言也厉。"

（十）

子夏曰："君子信而后劳其民。未信，则以为厉己也。信而后谏。未信，则以为谤己矣。"

（十一）

子夏曰："大德不逾闲，小德出入，可也。"

（十二）

子游曰："子夏之门人小子，当洒扫应对进退则可矣，抑末也。本之则无，如之何?" 子夏闻之，曰："噫! 言游过矣。君子之道，孰先传焉，孰后倦焉，譬诸草木，区以别矣。君子之道，焉可诬也? 有始有卒者，其惟圣人乎!"

9   Tzu-hsia said, A gentleman has three varying aspects: seen from afar, he looks severe, when approached he is found to be mild, when heard speaking he turns out to be incisive.

10 Tzu-hsia said, A gentleman obtains the confidence of those under him, before putting burdens upon them. If he does so before he has obtained their confidence, they feel that they are being exploited. It is also true that he obtains the confidence (of those above him) before criticising them. If he does so before he has obtained their confidence, they feel that they are being slandered.

11 Tzu-hsia said, So long as in undertakings of great moral import a man does not 'cross the barrier', in undertakings of little moral import he may 'come out and go in'. 1

12 Tzu-yu said, Tzu-hsia's disciples and scholars, so long as it is only a matter of sprinkling and sweeping floors, answering summonses and replying to questions, coming forward and retiring, are all right. But these are minor matters. Set them to anything important, and they would be quite at a loss.

Tzu-hsia, hearing of this, said, Alas, Yen Yu is wholly mistaken. Of the Way of the True Gentleman it is said:

> If it be transmitted to him before he is ripe
> By the time he is ripe, he will weary of it.

Disciples may indeed be compared to plants and trees. They have to be separately treated according to their kinds.

In the Way of the Gentleman there can be no bluff. It is only the Divine Sage who embraces in himself both the first step and the last.

1   In matters such as loyalty, keeping promises, obedience to parents, the laws which govern his conduct are absolute. In lesser matters he is allowed a certain latitude. Several early writers attribute the saying to Confucius himself.

(十三)

子夏曰：　"仕而优则学，学而优则仕。"

(十四)

子游曰：　"丧，致乎哀而止。"

(十五)

子游曰：　"吾友张也，为难能也，然而未仁。"

(十六)

曾子曰：　"堂堂乎张也，难与并为仁矣。"

(十七)

曾子曰：　"吾闻诸夫子，人未有自致者也，必也亲丧乎！"

(十八)

曾子曰：　"吾闻诸夫子，孟庄子之孝也，其他可能也，其不改父之臣与父之政，是难能也。"

(十九)

孟氏使阳肤为士师，问于曾子。曾子曰：　"上失其道，民散久矣。如得其情，则哀矜而勿喜。"

13 Tzu-hsia said, The energy that a man has left[1] over after doing his duty to the State, he should devote to study; the energy that he has left after studying, he should devote to service of the State.

14 Tzu-yu said, The ceremonies of mourning should be carried to the extreme that grief dictates, and no further.

15 Tzu-yu said, My friend Chang does 'the things that it is hard to be able to do';[2] but he is not yet Good.

16 Master Tsêng said, Chang is so self-important. It is hard to become Good when working side by side with such a man.

17 Master Tsêng said, I once heard the Master say, Though a man may never before have shown all that is in him, he is certain to do so when mourning for a father or mother.

18 Master Tsêng said, I once heard the Master say, Filial piety such as that of Mêng Chuang Tzu[3] might in other respects be possible to imitate; but the way in which he changed neither his father's[4] servants nor his father's domestic policy, that would indeed be hard to emulate.

19 When the Chief of the Mêng Family[5] appointed Yang Fu as Leader of the Knights,[6] Yang Fu[7] came for advice to Master Tsêng. Master Tsêng said, It is long since those above lost the Way of the Ruler and the common people lost their cohesion. If you find evidence of this, then be sad and show pity rather than be pleased at discovering such evidence.

1 cf. I, 6.
2 cf. XIV, 2.
3 Died in 550 BC.
4 Mêng Hsien Tzu, died in 554 BC.
5 Mêng Wu Po, who succeeded to the headship of the clan in 481 BC. Usually explained as meaning Mêng I Tzu, predecessor of Mêng Wu Po. But in his time (if we are to follow the traditional chronology) Master Tsêng would have been too young to be consulted. It must be remembered, however, that the Confucian legend was not built up by people who had chronological tables open in front of them.
6 A post involving the judging of criminal cases.
7 Unknown.

（二十）

子贡曰："纣之不善，不如是之甚也。是以君子恶居下流，天下之恶皆归焉。"

（二十一）

子贡曰："君子之过也，如日月之食焉。过也，人皆见之；更也，人皆仰之。"

（二十二）

卫公孙朝问于子贡曰："仲尼焉学？"子贡曰："文武之道，未坠于地，在人。贤者识其大者，不贤者识其小者，莫不有文武之道焉。夫子焉不学？而亦何常师之有？"

（二十三）

叔孙武叔语大夫于朝，曰："子贡贤于仲尼。"子服景伯以告子贡。子贡曰："譬之宫墙，赐之墙也及肩，窥见室家之好。夫子之墙数仞，不得其门而入，不见宗庙之美，百官之富。得其门者或寡矣。夫子之云，不亦宜乎？"

20 Tzu-kung said, The tyrant Chou[1] cannot really have been as wicked as all this! That is why a gentleman hates to 'dwell on low ground'. He knows that all filth under Heaven tends to accumulate there.

21 Tzu-kung said, The faults of a gentleman are like eclipses of the sun or moon. If he does wrong, everyone sees it. When he corrects his fault, every gaze is turned up towards him.

22 Kung-sun Ch'ao of Wei[2] asked Tzu-kung, From whom did Chung-ni[3] derive his learning? Tzu-kung said, The Way of the kings Wên and Wu has never yet utterly fallen to the ground. Among men,[4] those of great understanding have recorded the major principles of this Way and those of less understanding have recorded the minor principles. So that there is no one who has not access to the Way of Wên and Wu. From whom indeed did our Master *not* learn? But at the same time, what need had he of any fixed and regular teacher?

23 Shu-sun Wu-shu[5] talking to some high officers at Court said, Tzu-kung is a better man than Chung-ni. Tzu-fu Ching-po[6] repeated this to Tzu-kung. Tzu-kung said, Let us take as our comparison the wall round a building. My wall only reaches to the level of a man's shoulder, and it is easy enough to peep over it and see the good points of the house on the other side. But our Master's wall rises many times a man's height, and no one who is not let in by the gate can know the beauty and wealth of the palace that, with its ancestral temple, its hundred ministrants, lies hidden within. But it must be admitted that those who are let in by the gate are few; so that it is small wonder His Excellency should have spoken as he did.

1   See XVIII, 1.
2   So called to distinguish him from a number of Kung-sun Ch'aos in other countries.
3   i.e. Confucius.
4   The usual interpretation: 'It is still here among men', implies a very abrupt construction.
5   Flourished c.500 BC.
6   cf. XIV, 38.

(二十四)

叔孙武叔毁仲尼。子贡曰："无以为也，仲尼不可毁也。他人之贤者，丘陵也，犹可逾也。仲尼，日月也，无得而逾焉。人虽欲自绝，其何伤于日月乎？多见其不知量也。"

(二十五)

陈子禽谓子贡曰："子为恭也，仲尼岂贤于子乎？"子贡曰："君子一言以为智，一言以为不智，言不可不慎也。夫子之不可及也，犹天之不可阶而升也。夫子之得邦家者，所谓立之斯立，道之斯行，绥之斯来，动之斯和，其生也荣，其死也哀，如之何其可及也？"

24 Shu-sun Wu-shu having spoken disparagingly of Chung-ni, Tzu-kung said, It is no use; Chung-ni cannot be disparaged. There may be other good men; but they are merely like hillocks or mounds that can easily be climbed. Chung-ni is the sun and moon that cannot be climbed over. If a man should try to cut himself off from them, what harm would it do to the sun and moon? It would only show that he did not know his own measure.

25 Tzu-ch'in [1] said to Tzu-kung, This is an affectation of modesty. Chung-ni is in no way your superior. Tzu-kung said, You should be more careful about what you say. A gentleman, though for a single word he may be set down as wise, for a single word is set down as a fool. It would be as hard to equal our Master as to climb up on a ladder to the sky. Had our Master ever been put in control of a State or of a great Family, it would have been as is described in the words: 'He raised them, and they stood, he led them and they went. He steadied them as with a rope, and they came. He stirred them, and they moved harmoniously. His life was glorious, his death bewailed.' [2] How can such a one ever be equalled?

1 See I, 10 and XVI, 13.
2 Probably a quotation from a *lei* (funeral eulogy).

尧曰第二十

(一)

　　尧曰：　"咨，尔舜！天之历数在尔躬，允执其中，四海困穷，天禄永终。"舜亦以命禹。曰：　"予小子履，敢用玄牡，敢昭告于皇皇后帝。有罪不敢赦。帝臣不蔽，简在帝心。朕躬有罪，无以万方。万方有罪，

BOOK TWENTY

1   Yao said, Oh you, Shun!

> Upon you in your own person now rests the heavenly
>   succession; [1]
> Faithfully grasp it by the centre.
> The Four Seas may run dry; [2]
> But this heavenly gift lasts forever.

Shun too, when giving his charge to Yü . . . (hiatus).

(T'ang) [3] said, I, your little son Li, venture to sacrifice a black ox and tell you, oh most august sovereign God, that those who are guilty [4] I dare not spare; but God's servants I will not slay. The decision is in your heart, O God.

If I in my own person do any wrong, let it never be visited upon the many lands. But if anywhere in the many lands wrong be done, let it be visited upon my person. [5]

1   See additional notes.
2   i.e. 'sooner shall the sea run dry, than this gift . . . ' For *yung-chung*, cf. *Shu Ching*, Metal Casket, 10.
3   Founder of the Yin dynasty, when informing the Supreme Ancestor of his (T'ang's) accession. Li was his personal name.
4   The Hsia, whom T'ang had defeated.
5   This 'scape-goat' formula is constantly referred to in early Chinese literature. Mo Tzu (Universal Love, Pt. III), after quoting this same passage, says that T'ang 'did not scruple to make of himself a sacrificial victim'. The passage has been reinterpreted in a very drastic fashion.

在朕躬。"周有大赉，善人是富。"虽有周亲，不如仁人。百姓有过，在予一人。""谨权量，审法度，修废官，四方之政行焉。兴灭国，继绝世，举逸民，天下之民归心焉。"所重民食丧祭。"宽则得众，信则民任焉，敏则有功，公则说。"

(二)

子张问于孔子，曰："何如斯可以从政矣?"子曰："尊五美，屏四恶，斯可以从政矣。"子张曰："何谓五美?"子曰："君子惠而不费，劳而不怨，欲而不贪，泰而不骄，威而不猛。"子张曰："何谓惠而不

When Chou gave its great largesses,
It was the good who were enriched:
'Although I have my Chou kinsmen,
They are less to me than the Good Men.[1]
If among the many families
There be one that does wrong,
Let the wrong be visited on me alone.'

(King Wu)[2] paid strict attention to weights and measures, reviewed the statutes and laws, restored disused offices, and gave a polity to all the four quarters of the world. He raised up States that had been destroyed, re-established lines of succession that had been broken, summoned lost subjects back to prominence, and all the common people under Heaven gave their hearts to him. What he cared for most was that the people should have food, and that the rites of mourning and sacrifice should be fulfilled.

He who is broad[3] wins the multitude, he who keeps his word is trusted by the people, he who is diligent succeeds in all he undertakes, he who is just is the joy (of the people).

2   Tzu-chang asked Master K'ung, saying, What must a man do, that he may thereby be fitted to govern the land? The Master said, He must pay attention to the Five Lovely Things[4] and put away from him the Four Ugly Things. Tzu-chang said, What are they, that you call the Five Lovely Things? The Master said, A gentleman 'can be bounteous without extravagance, can get work out of people without arousing resentment, has longings but is never covetous, is proud but never insolent, inspires awe but is never ferocious'.

Tzu-chang said, What is meant by being bounteous without extravagance? The Master said, If he gives to the people only

1   i.e. those who distinguished themselves in the campaign against Yin. The speaker is presumably King Wu.
2   Or the Duke of Chou?
3   'He who is broad' down to 'undertakes' occurs also in XVII, 6.
4   For these enumerations, cf. XVI, 4-8.

费?" 子曰: "因民之所利而利之, 斯不亦惠而不费
乎? 择其可劳而劳之, 又谁怨? 欲仁而得仁, 又焉贪?
君子无众寡, 无小大, 无敢慢, 斯不亦泰而不骄乎? 君
子正其衣冠, 尊其瞻视, 俨然人望而畏之, 斯不亦威
而不猛乎?" 子张曰: "何谓四恶?" 子曰: "不教而
杀谓之虐。不戒视成谓之暴。慢令致期谓之贼。犹之
与人也, 出纳之吝, 谓之有司。"

(三)

孔子曰: "不知命, 无以为君子也。不知礼, 无
以立也。不知言, 无以知人也。"

such advantages as are really advantageous[1] to them, is he not being bounteous without extravagance? If he imposes upon them only such tasks as they are capable of performing, is he not getting work out of them without arousing resentment? If what he longs for and what he gets is Goodness, who can say that he is covetous? A gentleman, irrespective of whether he is dealing with many persons or with few, with the small or with the great, never presumes to slight them. Is not this indeed being 'proud without insolence'? A gentleman sees to it that his clothes and hat are put on straight, and imparts such dignity to his gaze that he imposes on others. No sooner do they see him from afar than they are in awe. Is not this indeed inspiring awe without ferocity?

Tzu-chang said, What are they, that you call the Four Ugly Things? The Master said, Putting men to death, without having taught them (the Right); that is called savagery. Expecting the completion of tasks, without giving due warning; that is called oppression. To be dilatory about giving orders, but to expect absolute punctuality, that is called being a tormentor. And similarly, though meaning to let a man have something, to be grudging about bringing it out from within, that is called behaving like a petty functionary.

3   The Master said, He who does not understand the will of Heaven cannot be regarded as a gentleman. He who does not know the rites cannot take his stand.[2] He who does not understand words,[3] cannot understand people.

---

1   For example, if he promotes agriculture instead of distributing doles and largesses.

2   cf. XVI, 13.

3   i.e. cannot get beneath the surface-meaning and understand the state of mind that the words really imply. cf. *Mencius*, II, A, 2. Para. 3 was lacking in the Lu version.